THE YALE SHAKESPEARE

Edited by

Wilbur L. Cross   Tucker Brooke
Willard Higley Durham

Published under the Direction
of the
Department of English, Yale University
on the Fund
Given to the Yale University Press in 1917
by the Members of the
Kingsley Trust Association
To Commemorate the Seventy-Fifth Anniversary
of the Founding of the Society

·: The Yale Shakespeare :·

THE TRAGEDY OF JULIUS CÆSAR

EDITED BY

LAWRENCE MASON

NEW HAVEN · YALE UNIVERSITY PRESS
LONDON · OXFORD UNIVERSITY PRESS

TABLE OF CONTENTS

The facsimile opposite represents page two in Mr. William A. White's copy of the fifth quarto edition. Three copies of this edition are known to survive.

Dramatis Personæ.

MEN.

	Julius Cæsar	Mr. *Goodman.*
	Octavius Cæsar	Mr. *Perrin.*
	Antony	Mr. *Kynaston.*
	Brutus	Mr. *Betterton.*
	Cassius	Mr. *Smith.*
	Caska	Mr. *Griffin.*
Conspirators	Trebonius	Mr. *Saunders,*
against	Ligarius	Mr. *Bowman.*
Cæsar.	Decius Brutus	Mr. *Williams.*
	Metellus Cimber	Mr. *Mountfort.*
	Cinna	Mr. *Carlisle.*
	Flavius	Mr. *Norris.*
	Murellus	Mr.
	Artemidorus	Mr. *Percival.*
Friends to	Messala	Mr. *Wiltshire.*
Brutus.	Titinius	Mr. *Gillo.*
	Cinna *the Poet*	Mr. *Jevon.*
	Lucius *Servant to* Brutus }	Mr.
		Mr. *Underhill.*
	Plebeians }	Mr. *Lee.*
		Mr. *Bright.*

WOMEN.

Calphurnia	Md. *Slingsby.*
Portia	Mrs. *Cook.*

GUARDS and ATTENDANTS.

SCENE, *for the Three first Acts, and Beginning of the Fourth,* in Rome; *for the Remainder of the Fourth, near* Sardis; *for the Fifth, in the Fields of* Philippi.

[DRAMATIS PERSONÆ

JULIUS CÆSAR

OCTAVIUS CÆSAR,
MARCUS ANTONIUS,
M. ÆMILIUS LEPIDUS, } *Triumvirs after the Death of Julius Cæsar*

CICERO,
PUBLIUS,
POPILIUS LENA, } *Senators*

MARCUS BRUTUS,
CAIUS CASSIUS,
CASCA,
TREBONIUS,
LIGARIUS,
DECIUS BRUTUS,
METELLUS CIMBER,
CINNA, } *Conspirators against Julius Cæsar*

FLAVIUS and MARULLUS, *Tribunes*
ARTEMIDORUS, *a Sophist of Cnidos*
A Soothsayer
CINNA, *a Poet*
Another Poet

LUCILIUS,
TITINIUS,
MESSALA,
YOUNG CATO,
VOLUMNIUS, } *Friends to Brutus and Cassius*

VARRO,
CLITUS,
CLAUDIUS,
STRATO,
LUCIUS,
DARDANIUS, } *Servants to Brutus*

PINDARUS, *Servant to Cassius*

CALPURNIA, *Wife to Cæsar*
PORTIA, *Wife to Brutus*

Commoners, or Plebeians, of Rome; Senators, Guards, Attendants, etc.

SCENE: *Act I-Act IV, Scene i, at Rome; Act IV, Scenes ii and iii, near Sardis, in Asia Minor; Act V, the plains near Philippi, in Macedonia.*]

The Tragedy of Julius Cæsar

ACT FIRST

Scene One

[*Rome. A Street*]

*Enter Flavius, Marullus, and certain Commoners over
the Stage.*

Flav. Hence! home, you idle creatures, get you
home:
Is this a holiday? What! know you not,
Being mechanical, you ought not walk
Upon a labouring day without the sign   4
Of your profession? Speak, what trade art thou?

Car. Why, sir, a carpenter.

Mar. Where is thy leather apron, and thy rule?
What dost thou with thy best apparel on?   8
You, sir, what trade are you?

Cob. Truly, sir, in respect of a fine workman,
I am but, as you would say, a cobbler.

Mar. But what trade art thou? Answer me directly.   12

Cob. A trade, sir, that, I hope, I may use
with a safe conscience; which is, indeed, sir, a
mender of bad soles.

Mar. What trade, thou knave? thou naughty knave,
what trade?   16

Scene One S. d. Marullus; *cf. n.*
3 mechanical: *of the laboring class*   walk: *go about the streets*
4, 5 sign . . . profession: *artisan's garb and implements*
10 in respect of: *in comparison with*   11 cobbler: *bungler*
12 directly: *plainly, without evasion*   16 naughty: *wicked, worthless*

Cob. Nay, I beseech you, sir, be not out with
me: yet, if you be out, sir, I can mend you.

Mar. What mean'st thou by that? Mend
me, thou saucy fellow?   20

Cob. Why, sir, cobble you.

Flav. Thou art a cobbler, art thou?

Cob. Truly, sir, all that I live by is with
the awl: I meddle with no tradesman's matters,
nor women's matters, but with awl. I am, in- 25
deed, sir, a surgeon to old shoes; when they are
in great danger, I recover them. As proper men
as ever trod upon neat's leather have gone upon
my handiwork.   29

Flav. But wherefore art not in thy shop to-day?
Why dost thou lead these men about the streets?

Cob. Truly, sir, to wear out their shoes,
to get myself into more work. But, indeed, sir,
we make holiday to see Cæsar and to rejoice in
his triumph.

Mar. Wherefore rejoice? What conquest brings
he home?   36
What tributaries follow him to Rome
To grace in captive bonds his chariot wheels?
You blocks, you stones, you worse than senseless
    things!
O you hard hearts, you cruel men of Rome,   40
Knew you not Pompey? Many a time and oft
Have you climb'd up to walls and battlements,
To towers and windows, yea, to chimney-tops,
Your infants in your arms, and there have sat   44
The livelong day, with patient expectation,
To see great Pompey pass the streets of Rome:

17 out: *out of temper*   18 be out: *have hole in shoe*
25 with awl; *cf. n.*
28 neat's leather: *cowhide*   27 proper: *goodly, worthy*
                                        35 triumph; *cf. n.*

And when you saw his chariot but appear,
Have you not made a universal shout,   48
That Tiber trembled underneath her banks,
To hear the replication of your sounds
Made in her concave shores?
And do you now put on your best attire?   52
And do you now cull out a holiday?
And do you now strew flowers in his way,
That comes in triumph over Pompey's blood?
Be gone!   56
Run to your houses, fall upon your knees,
Pray to the gods to intermit the plague
That needs must light on this ingratitude.

    Flav. Go, go, good countrymen, and for this
      fault   60
Assemble all the poor men of your sort;
Draw them to Tiber banks, and weep your tears
Into the channel, till the lowest stream
Do kiss the most exalted shores of all.   64

               Exeunt all the Commoners.

See whether their basest metal be not mov'd;
They vanish tongue-tied in their guiltiness.
Go you down that way towards the Capitol;
This way will I.   Disrobe the images   68
If you do find them deck'd with ceremonies.

    Mar. May we do so?
You know it is the feast of Lupercal.

    Flav. It is no matter; let no images   72
Be hung with Cæsar's trophies.   I'll about
And drive away the vulgar from the streets:
So do you too where you perceive them thick.

---

49 her; *cf. n.*   50 replication: *echo*
53 cull out: *choose this as*   55 Pompey's blood; *cf. n. on line 35*
69 ceremonies: *ceremonial trappings*   71 Lupercal; *cf. n.*

These   growing   feathers   pluck'd   from   Cæsar's
    wing   76
Will make him fly an ordinary pitch,
Who else would soar above the view of men
And keep us all in servile fearfulness.   *Exeunt.*

Scene Two

[A Public Place]

*Enter [in solemn procession, with music] Cæsar, An-
tony for the course, Calpurnia, Portia, Decius,
Cicero, Brutus, Cassius, Casca, [a great crowd
following, among them] a Soothsayer: after them
Marullus and Flavius.*

   Cæs. Calpurnia!
   Casca.   Peace, ho! Cæsar speaks.
                                      [Music ceases.]
   Cæs.   Calpurnia!
   Cal. Here, my lord.
   Cæs. Stand you directly in Antonius' way
When he doth run his course.   Antonius!   4
   Ant. Cæsar, my lord.
   Cæs. Forget not, in your speed, Antonius,
To touch Calpurnia; for our elders say,
The barren, touched in this holy chase,   8
Shake off their sterile curse.
   Ant.   I shall remember:
When Cæsar says 'Do this,' it is perform'd.
   Cæs. Set on; and leave no ceremony out.   *[Music.]*
   Sooth. Cæsar!   12
   Cæs. Ha!   Who calls?

---

77 pitch: *height, as of a hawk's flight*   6 in . . . speed: *as you run*
9 sterile curse: *affliction of barrenness*   11 Set on: *proceed, advance*

Casca. Bid every noise be still: peace yet again!

                               [*Music ceases.*]

Cæs. Who is it in the press that calls on me?

I hear a tongue, shriller than all the music,   **16**

Cry 'Cæsar.' Speak; Cæsar is turn'd to hear.

Sooth. Beware the ides of March.

Cæs.   What man is that?

Bru. A soothsayer bids you beware the ides of
   March.

Cæs. Set him before me; let me see his face.   **20**

Cas. Fellow, come from the throng; look upon
   Cæsar.

Cæs. What sayst thou to me now? Speak once
   again.

Sooth. Beware the ides of March.

Cæs. He is a dreamer; let us leave him: pass.   **24**

      Sennet. Exeunt all but Brutus and Cassius.

Cas. Will you go see the order of the course?

Bru. Not I.

Cas. I pray you, do.

Bru. I am not gamesome: I do lack some part   **28**

Of that quick spirit that is in Antony.

Let me not hinder, Cassius, your desires;

I'll leave you.

Cas. Brutus, I do observe you now of late: **32**

I have not from your eyes that gentleness

And show of love as I was wont to have:

You bear too stubborn and too strange a hand

Over your friend that loves you.

Bru.   Cassius,   **36**

---

18 ides of March: *March fifteenth*
24 S. d. Sennet: *trumpet signal for procession to move*
25 order of the course: *progress of the running*
28 gamesome: *fond of sport*   29 quick: *lively*
32 do observe: *have had occasion to notice*   33 that: *the same*
35, 36 *handle your friend too stiffly and distantly*

Be not deceiv'd: if I have veil'd my look,
I turn the trouble of my countenance
Merely upon myself. Vexed I am
Of late with passions of some difference,   40
Conceptions only proper to myself,
Which give some soil perhaps to my behaviours;
But let not therefore my good friends be griev'd,—
Among which number, Cassius, be you one,—   44
Nor construe any further my neglect,
Than that poor Brutus, with himself at war,
Forgets the shows of love to other men.

   Cas. Then, Brutus, I have much mistook your
      passion;   48
By means whereof this breast of mine hath buried
Thoughts of great value, worthy cogitations.
Tell me, good Brutus, can you see your face?

   Bru. No, Cassius; for the eye sees not itself,   52
But by reflection, by some other things.

   Cas. 'Tis just:
And it is very much lamented, Brutus,
That you have no such mirrors as will turn   56
Your hidden worthiness into your eye,
That you might see your shadow. I have heard
Where many of the best respect in Rome,—
Except immortal Cæsar,—speaking of Brutus,   60
And groaning underneath this age's yoke,
Have wish'd that noble Brutus had his eyes.

   Bru. Into what dangers would you lead me, Cassius,
That you would have me seek into myself   64
For that which is not in me?

   Cas. Therefore, good Brutus, be prepar'd to hear;

---

37 Be not deceiv'd: *do not misjudge me*   39 Merely: *altogether*
40 of . . . difference: *conflicting*   41 proper: *belonging, relating*
42 soil: *blemish*   45 construe: *read meaning into*
49 By . . . whereof: *because of which mistake*   54 just: *true, right*
59 respect: *standing*   62 had . . . eyes: *had his eyes about him*

And, since you know you cannot see yourself
So well as by reflection, I, your glass,   68
Will modestly discover to yourself
That of yourself which you yet know not of.
And be not jealous on me, gentle Brutus:
Were I a common laugher, or did use   72
To stale with ordinary oaths my love
To every new protester; if you know
That I do fawn on men and hug them hard,
And after scandal them; or if you know   76
That I profess myself in banqueting
To all the rout, then hold me dangerous.

                                    Flourish, and shout.

  Bru. What means this shouting? I do fear the
    people
Choose Cæsar for their king.
  Cas.   Ay, do you fear it?   80
Then must I think you would not have it so.
  Bru. I would not, Cassius; yet I love him well.
But wherefore do you hold me here so long?
What is it that you would impart to me?   84
If it be aught toward the general good,
Set honour in one eye and death i' the other,
And I will look on both indifferently;
For let the gods so speed me as I love   88
The name of honour more than I fear death.

  Cas. I know that virtue to be in you, Brutus,
As well as I do know your outward favour.
Well, honour is the subject of my story.   92
I cannot tell what you and other men

---

71 jealous on: *suspicious of*
73 stale: *make cheap*   ordinary: *customary*
74 protester: *loud-mouthed pretender*
76 scandal: *defame*   77 profess myself: *make protestations*
78 S. d. Flourish: *trumpet call*   87 indifferently: *impartially*
88 speed: *favor, prosper*   91 favour: *appearance*

Think of this life; but, for my single self,
I had as lief not be as live to be
In awe of such a thing as I myself.   96
I was born free as Cæsar; so were you:
We both have fed as well, and we can both
Endure the winter's cold as well as he:
For once, upon a raw and gusty day,   100
The troubled Tiber chafing with her shores,
Cæsar said to me, 'Dar'st thou, Cassius, now
Leap in with me into this angry flood,
And swim to yonder point?' Upon the word,   104
Accoutred as I was, I plunged in
And bade him follow; so, indeed he did.
The torrent roar'd, and we did buffet it
With lusty sinews, throwing it aside   108
And stemming it with hearts of controversy;
But ere we could arrive the point propos'd,
Cæsar cried, 'Help me, Cassius, or I sink!'
I, as Æneas, our great ancestor,   112
Did from the flames of Troy upon his shoulder
The old Anchises bear, so from the waves of Tiber
Did I the tired Cæsar. And this man
Is now become a god, and Cassius is   116
A wretched creature and must bend his body
If Cæsar carelessly but nod on him.
He had a fever when he was in Spain,
And when the fit was on him, I did mark   120
How he did shake; 'tis true, this god did shake;
His coward lips did from their colour fly,
And that same eye whose bend doth awe the world
Did lose his lustre; I did hear him groan;   124

101 with: *against*
105 Accoutred: *clad*
109 hearts of controversy: *contesting courage*
122 *his lips forsook their normal redness as cowardly soldiers forsake
    their flag*   123 bend: *glance*   124 his: *its*

Ay, and that tongue of his that bade the Romans
Mark him and write his speeches in their books,
Alas! it cried, 'Give me some drink, Titinius',
As a sick girl. Ye gods, it doth amaze me,   128
A man of such a feeble temper should
So get the start of the majestic world,
And bear the palm alone.   *Shout. Flourish.*
    Bru.   Another general shout!
I do believe that these applauses are   132
For some new honours that are heap'd on Cæsar.
    Cas. Why, man, he doth bestride the narrow world
Like a Colossus; and we petty men
Walk under his huge legs, and peep about   136
To find ourselves dishonourable graves.
Men at some time are masters of their fates:
The fault, dear Brutus, is not in our stars,
But in ourselves, that we are underlings.   140
Brutus and Cæsar: what should be in that 'Cæsar'?
Why should that name be sounded more than yours?
Write them together, yours is as fair a name;
Sound them, it doth become the mouth as well;   144
Weigh them, it is as heavy; conjure with 'em,
'Brutus' will start a spirit as soon as 'Cæsar'.
Now, in the names of all the gods at once,
Upon what meat doth this our Cæsar feed,   148
That he is grown so great? Age, thou art sham'd!
Rome, thou hast lost the breed of noble bloods!
When went there by an age, since the great flood,
But it was fam'd with more than with one man?   152
When could they say, till now, that talk'd of Rome,

129 temper: *constitution*
130 get the start of: *outstrip (in the race of life)*
135 Colossus: *gigantic statue astride the mouth of the harbor of Rhodes*
150 lost . . . bloods: *lost the art of breeding noble persons*
151 the great flood: *Deucalion's, not Noah's*
152 fam'd with: *famous for*

That her wide walks encompass'd but one man?
Now is it Rome indeed and room enough,
When there is in it but one only man.   156
O, you and I have heard our fathers say,
There was a Brutus once that would have brook'd
Th' eternal devil to keep his state in Rome
As easily as a king.   160

   Bru. That you do love me, I am nothing jealous;
What you would work me to, I have some aim:
How I have thought of this and of these times,
I shall recount hereafter; for this present,   164
I would not, so with love I might entreat you,
Be any further mov'd. What you have said
I will consider; what you have to say
I will with patience hear, and find a time   168
Both meet to hear and answer such high things.
Till then, my noble friend, chew upon this:
Brutus had rather be a villager
Than to repute himself a son of Rome   172
Under these hard conditions as this time
Is like to lay upon us.

   Cas.   I am glad
That my weak words have struck but thus much show
Of fire from Brutus.   176

   Bru. The games are done and Cæsar is returning.

   Cas. As they pass by, pluck Casca by the sleeve,
And he will, after his sour fashion, tell you
What hath proceeded worthy note to-day.   180

        Enter Cæsar and his Train.

154 walks; *cf. n.*   155 Rome: *then often pronounced 'Room'*
158 Brutus: *Lucius Junius, who expelled the Tarquins, ca. 510 B. C.*
    brook'd: *tolerated*   159 state: *throne, rulership*
161 nothing: *not at all*   jealous: *doubtful*
162 work: *induce*   aim: *inkling*
165 so: *if; cf. n.*   166 mov'd: *persuaded, urged*
169 meet: *fit*   170 chew: *ponder*   173 as: *such as*

Bru. I will do so. But, look you, Cassius,
The angry spot doth glow on Cæsar's brow,
And all the rest look like a chidden train:
Calpurnia's cheek is pale, and Cicero   184
Looks with such ferret and such fiery eyes
As we have seen him in the Capitol,
Being cross'd in conference by some senators.
   Cas. Casca will tell us what the matter is.   188
   Cæs. Antonius!
   Ant. Cæsar.
   Cæs. Let me have men about me that are fat;
Sleek-headed men and such as sleep o' nights.   192
Yond Cassius has a lean and hungry look;
He thinks too much: such men are dangerous.
   Ant. Fear him not, Cæsar, he's not dangerous;
He is a noble Roman, and well given.   196
   Cæs. Would he were fatter! but I fear him not:
Yet if my name were liable to fear,
I do not know the man I should avoid
So soon as that spare Cassius. He reads much;   200
He is a great observer, and he looks
Quite through the deeds of men; he loves no plays,
As thou dost, Antony; he hears no music;
Seldom he smiles, and smiles in such a sort   204
As if he mock'd himself, and scorn'd his spirit
That could be mov'd to smile at anything.
Such men as he be never at heart's ease
Whiles they behold a greater than themselves,   208
And therefore are they very dangerous.
I rather tell thee what is to be fear'd
Than what I fear, for always I am Cæsar.

185 ferret: *ferret-like, i.e., small and red*
187 conference: *debate*
192 Sleek-headed: *unruffled by deep plotting*
196 well given: *well disposed*   198 my name; *cf. n.*
203 he . . . music; *cf. n.*   208 Whiles: *whilst, while*

Come on my right hand, for this ear is deaf,   212
And tell me truly what thou think'st of him.

    Sennet. Exeunt Cæsar and his Train [except
                     Casca].

 Casca. You pull'd me by the cloak; would you
  speak with me?

 Bru. Ay, Casca; tell us what hath chanc'd to-day,
That Cæsar looks so sad.   216

 Casca. Why, you were with him, were you not?

 Bru. I should not then ask Casca what had chanc'd.

 Casca. Why, there was a crown offered him;
and, being offered him, he put it by with the 220
back of his hand, thus; and then the people fell
a-shouting.

 Bru. What was the second noise for?

 Casca.   Why, for that too.   224

 Cas. They shouted thrice: what was the last cry
for?

 Casca. Why, for that too.

 Bru. Was the crown offered him thrice?   227

 Casca. Ay, marry, was 't, and he put it by
thrice, every time gentler than other; and at every
putting-by mine honest neighbours shouted.

 Cas. Who offered him the crown?

 Casca.   Why, Antony.   232

 Bru. Tell us the manner of it, gentle Casca.

 Casca. I can as well be hanged as tell the
manner of it: it was mere foolery; I did not
mark it. I saw Mark Antony offer him a crown;
yet 'twas not a crown neither, 'twas one of these
coronets; and, as I told you, he put it by once; 238
but, for all that, to my thinking, he would fain

216 sad: *grave, serious*
228 marry: *properly an invocation of the Virgin*
238 coronets: *laurel garland of a Lupercal runner*

have had it. Then he offered it to him again;
then he put it by again; but, to my thinking, he
was very loath to lay his fingers off it. And then
he offered it the third time; he put it the third
time by; and still as he refused it the rabblement
shouted and clapped their chopped hands, and 245
threw up their sweaty night-caps, and uttered
such a deal of stinking breath because Cæsar
refused the crown, that it had almost choked
Cæsar; for he swounded and fell down at it: and
for mine own part, I durst not laugh, for fear of
opening my lips and receiving the bad air.

Cas. But soft, I pray you: what! did Cæsar
    swound?   252

  Casca. He fell down in the market-place, and
foamed at mouth, and was speechless.

Bru. 'Tis very like: he hath the falling-sickness.

Cas. No, Cæsar hath it not; but you, and I,
And honest Casca, we have the falling-sickness.

  Casca. I know not what you mean by that; 258
but I am sure Cæsar fell down. If the tag-rag
people did not clap him and hiss him, according
as he pleased and displeased them, as they use
to do the players in the theatre, I am no true
man.   263

Bru. What said he, when he came unto himself?

  Casca. Marry, before he fell down, when he
perceiv'd the common herd was glad he refused
the crown, he plucked me ope his doublet and
offered them his throat to cut. An I had been a 268

244 still: *always, ever*   245 chopped: *chapped, callous*
249 swounded: *fainted*   252 soft: *stop, wait*
255 like: *likely*   falling-sickness: *epilepsy*
259 tag-rag: *beggarly, common*
262 true: *honest*
267 me: *expletive 'dative of interest'*   ope: *open*   doublet: *Elisa-*
    bethan jacket   268 An: *if*

man of any occupation, if I would not have taken
him at a word, I would I might go to hell among
the rogues. And so he fell. When he came to
himself again, he said, if he had done or said
anything amiss, he desired their worships to 273
think it was his infirmity. Three or four
wenches, where I stood, cried, 'Alas, good soul!'
and forgave him with all their hearts: but
there's no heed to be taken of them; if Cæsar
had stabbed their mothers, they would have
done no less. 279

Bru. And after that he came, thus sad, away?

Casca. Ay.

Cas. Did Cicero say anything?

Casca. Ay, he spoke Greek.

Cas. To what effect? 284

Casca. Nay, an I tell you that, I'll ne'er look
you i' the face again; but those that understood
him smiled at one another and shook their
heads; but, for mine own part, it was Greek to
me. I could tell you more news too; Marullus
and Flavius, for pulling scarfs off Cæsar's images,
are put to silence. Fare you well. There was
more foolery yet, if I could remember it. 292

Cas. Will you sup with me to-night, Casca?

Casca. No, I am promised forth.

Cas. Will you dine with me to-morrow?

Casca. Ay, if I be alive, and your mind hold,
and your dinner worth the eating. 297

Cas. Good; I will expect you.

Casca. Do so. Farewell, both. *Exit.*

269 occupation: *artisan's calling*
291 put to silence: *dismissed, not killed*
294 *I have a previous engagement* (*to dine out*)

   Bru. What a blunt fellow is this grown to be!   300
He was quick mettle when he went to school.

   Cas. So is he now in execution
Of any bold or noble enterprise,
However he puts on this tardy form.   304
This rudeness is a sauce to his good wit,
Which gives men stomach to digest his words
With better appetite.

   Bru. And so it is. For this time I will leave
     you: 308
To-morrow, if you please to speak with me,
I will come home to you; or, if you will,
Come home to me, and I will wait for you.

   Cas. I will do so: till then, think of the world.   312
                                        Exit Brutus.
Well, Brutus, thou art noble; yet, I see,
Thy honourable metal may be wrought
From that it is dispos'd: therefore 'tis meet
That noble minds keep ever with their likes;   316
For who so firm that cannot be seduc'd?
Cæsar doth bear me hard; but he loves Brutus:
If I were Brutus now and he were Cassius,
He should not humour me. I will this night,   320
In several hands, in at his windows throw,
As if they came from several citizens,
Writings all tending to the great opinion
That Rome holds of his name; wherein obscurely   324
Cæsar's ambition shall be glanced at:
And after this let Cæsar seat him sure;
For we will shake him, or worse days endure.   *Exit.*

301 quick mettle: *high-spirited*
304 However: *notwithstanding that*   tardy form: *sluggish manner*
312 the world: *public affairs*   315 that: *that to which*
318 bear me hard: *dislike me*   320 He . . . me; *cf. n.*
321 several hands: *different handwritings*
327 or . . . endure: *or suffer disastrous consequences of our attempt*

Scene Three

[*A Street*]

Thunder and lightning.   Enter [from opposite sides]
    Casca [with his sword drawn] and Cicero.

Cic. Good even, Casca: brought you Cæsar home?
Why are you breathless? and why stare you so?

Casca. Are not you mov'd, when all the sway of
        earth
Shakes like a thing unfirm?   O Cicero!   4
I have seen tempests, when the scolding winds
Have riv'd the knotty oaks; and I have seen
The ambitious ocean swell and rage and foam,
To be exalted with the threat'ning clouds: 8
But never till to-night, never till now,
Did I go through a tempest dropping fire.
Either there is a civil strife in heaven,
Or else the world, too saucy with the gods,   12
Incenses them to send destruction.

Cic. Why, saw you anything more wonderful?

Casca. A common slave—you know him well by
        sight—
Held up his left hand, which did flame and burn   16
Like twenty torches join'd; and yet his hand,
Not sensible of fire, remain'd unscorch'd.
Besides,—I have not since put up my sword,—
Against the Capitol I met a lion,   20
Who glar'd upon me, and went surly by,
Without annoying me; and there were drawn
Upon a heap a hundred ghastly women,
Transformed with their fear, who swore they saw   24

---

1 brought: *escorted*   3 sway: *settled order*
14 more: *else (or, extraordinarily)*
18 sensible of: *vulnerable by, sensitive to*
22, 23 drawn . . . heap: *crowded together in a body*

Men all in fire walk up and down the streets.
And yesterday the bird of night did sit,
Even at noon-day, upon the market-place,
Hooting and shrieking. When these prodigies   28
Do so conjointly meet, let not men say,
'These are their reasons, they are natural';
For, I believe, they are portentous things
Unto the climate that they point upon.   32

   Cic. Indeed, it is a strange-disposed time:
But men may construe things after their fashion,
Clean from the purpose of the things themselves.
Comes Cæsar to the Capitol to-morrow?   36

   Casca. He doth; for he did bid Antonius
Send word to you he would be there to-morrow.

   Cic. Good-night then, Casca: this disturbed sky
Is not to walk in.

   Casca.   Farewell, Cicero.   40

                             Exit Cicero.
              Enter Cassius.

   Cas. Who's there?

   Casca.   A Roman.

   Cas.   Casca, by your voice.

   Casca. Your ear is good. Cassius, what night is
   this!

   Cas. A very pleasing night to honest men.

   Casca. Who ever knew the heavens menace so?   44

   Cas. Those that have known the earth so full of
   faults.
For my part, I have walk'd about the streets,
Submitting me unto the perilous night,

26 bird of night: *owl*
32 climate: *clime, region*   point upon: *apply to*
33 strange-disposed: *of strange character*
34 after . . . fashion: *according to men's own human predilection*
35 Clean . . . purpose: *quite apart from the true meaning*
39 sky: *air, state of weather*   42 what night: *what a night*

And, thus unbraced, Casca, as you see,   48
Have bar'd my bosom to the thunder-stone;
And, when the cross blue lightning seem'd to open
The breast of heaven, I did present myself
Even in the aim and very flash of it.   52
   Casca. But wherefore did you so much tempt the
     heavens?
It is the part of men to fear and tremble
When the most mighty gods by tokens send
Such dreadful heralds to astonish us.   56
   Cas. You are dull, Casca, and those sparks of life
That should be in a Roman you do want,
Or else you use not. You look pale, and gaze,
And put on fear, and cast yourself in wonder,   60
To see the strange impatience of the heavens;
But if you would consider the true cause
Why all these fires, why all these gliding ghosts,
Why birds and beasts, from quality and kind,   64
Why old men, fools, and children calculate,
Why all these things change from their ordinance,
Their natures, and pre-formed faculties,
To monstrous quality,—why, you shall find   68
That heaven hath infus'd them with these spirits
To make them instruments of fear and warning
Unto some monstrous state.
Now could I, Casca, name to thee a man   72
Most like this dreadful night,
That thunders, lightens, opens graves, and roars
As doth the lion in the Capitol,
A man no mightier than thyself or me   76

48 unbraced: *with doublet open*
49 thunder-stone: *supposedly cast from the sky by thunder*
60 put on: *exhibit the signs of*   cast . . . in: *give way to; cf. n.*
63 Why: *i.e., why we have* (*or*, . . . *are acting so*)
64 from . . . kind: *far from their proper character and nature*
65 calculate: *prophesy; cf. n.*   66 ordinance: *ordinary conduct*
71 monstrous state: *unnatural state of affairs*

In personal action, yet prodigious grown
And fearful as these strange eruptions are.

Casca. 'Tis Cæsar that you mean; is it not, Cassius?

Cas. Let it be who it is: for Romans now   80
Have thews and limbs like to their ancestors;
But, woe the while! our fathers' minds are dead,
And we are govern'd with our mothers' spirits;
Our yoke and sufferance show us womanish.   84

Casca. Indeed, they say the senators to-morrow
Mean to establish Cæsar as a king;
And he shall wear his crown by sea and land,
In every place, save here in Italy.   88

Cas. I know where I will wear this dagger then;
Cassius from bondage will deliver Cassius:
Therein, ye gods, you make the weak most strong;
Therein, ye gods, you tyrants do defeat: 92
Nor stony tower, nor walls of beaten brass,
Nor airless dungeon, nor strong links of iron,
Can be retentive to the strength of spirit:
But life, being weary of these worldly bars,   96
Never lacks power to dismiss itself.
If I know this, know all the world besides,
That part of tyranny that I do bear
I can shake off at pleasure.   *Thunder still.*

Casca.   So can I: 100
So every bondman in his own hand bears
The power to cancel his captivity.

Cas. And why should Cæsar be a tyrant then?
Poor man! I know he would not be a wolf   104
But that he sees the Romans are but sheep;

---

78 fearful: *inspiring fear*   eruptions: *freaks of nature*
82 woe the while: *alas for the times*
84 yoke and sufferance: *patience under the yoke*

He were no lion, were not Romans hinds.
Those that with haste will make a mighty fire
Begin it with weak straws; what trash is Rome,   108
What rubbish, and what offal, when it serves
For the base matter to illuminate
So vile a thing as Cæsar! But, O grief,
Where hast thou led me? I, perhaps, speak this   112
Before a willing bondman; then I know
My answer must be made: but I am arm'd,
And dangers are to me indifferent.

   Casca. You speak to Casca, and to such a man   116
That is no fleering tell-tale. Hold, my hand:
Be factious for redress of all these griefs,
And I will set this foot of mine as far
As who goes furthest.

   Cas.   There's a bargain made.   120
Now know you, Casca, I have mov'd already
Some certain of the noblest-minded Romans
To undergo with me an enterprise
Of honourable-dangerous consequence;   124
And I do know by this they stay for me
In Pompey's porch: for now, this fearful night,
There is no stir, or walking in the streets;
And the complexion of the element   128
In favour's like the work we have in hand,
Most bloody, fiery, and most terrible.

   Casca. Stand close awhile, for here comes one in
     haste.

106 hinds: *female of red deer; also, servants, rustics*
107-111 *Cf. n.*
114 My . . . made: *I shall have to answer for my words*
117 That: *as*   fleering: *mocking*   Hold, my hand: *here, take this*
    handclasp as pledge
118 factious: *active*   griefs: *grievances*
123 undergo: *undertake*   125 by this: *by this time*
126 Pompey's porch; *cf. n.*
128 complexion . . . element: *visible condition of the sky*
131 Stand close: *avoid notice*

Cas. 'Tis Cinna; I do know him by his gait:
He is a friend.

Enter Cinna.

Cinna, where haste you so?   **133**

Cin. To find out you. Who's that? Metellus
     Cimber?

Cas. No, it is Casca; one incorporate
To our attempts. Am I not stay'd for, Cinna?

Cin. I am glad on 't. What a fearful night is
     this!   **137**
There's two or three of us have seen strange sights.

Cas. Am I not stay'd for? Tell me.

Cin.   Yes, you are.
O Cassius, if you could   **140**
But win the noble Brutus to our party—

Cas. Be you content. Good Cinna, take this paper,
And look you lay it in the prætor's chair,
Where Brutus may but find it; and throw this   **144**
In at his window; set this up with wax
Upon old Brutus' statue: all this done,
Repair to Pompey's porch, where you shall find us.
Is Decius Brutus and Trebonius there?   **148**

Cin. All but Metellus Cimber; and he's gone
To seek you at your house. Well, I will hie,
And so bestow these papers as you bade me.

Cas. That done, repair to Pompey's theatre.   **152**

Exit Cinna.

Come, Casca, you and I will yet ere day
See Brutus at his house: three parts of him
Is ours already, and the man entire
Upon the next encounter yields him ours.   **156**

Casca. O, he sits high in all the people's hearts:

---

135 incorporate: *joined, affiliated*
143 prætor's chair: *official seat of judge in Roman tribunal*
150 hie: *hasten away*

And that which would appear offence in us,
His countenance, like richest alchemy,
Will change to virtue and to worthiness.   160
 Cas. Him and his worth and our great need of him
You have right well conceited. Let us go,
For it is after midnight; and ere day
We will awake him and be sure of him.   164
          Exeunt.

ACT SECOND

Scene One

Enter Brutus in his Orchard.

 Bru. What, Lucius! ho!
I cannot, by the progress of the stars,
Give guess how near to day. Lucius, I say!
I would it were my fault to sleep so soundly.   4
When, Lucius, when? Awake, I say! what, Lucius!

Enter Lucius.

 Luc. Call'd you, my lord?
 Bru. Get me a taper in my study, Lucius:
When it is lighted, come and call me here.   8
 Luc. I will, my lord.   *Exit.*
 Bru. It must be by his death: and, for my part,
I know no personal cause to spurn at him,
But for the general. He would be crown'd: 12
How that might change his nature, there's the question:
It is the bright day that brings forth the adder;

---

159 countenance: *patronage, support*   alchemy: *pseudo-science of*
  transmuting metals   162 conceited: *expressed figuratively*
Scene One S. d. Orchard: *garden*
5 When: *exclamation of impatience*
11 spurn at: *oppose vindictively*
12 general: *people's sake, public welfare*

And that craves wary walking. Crown him that,
And then, I grant, we put a sting in him   16
That at his will he may do danger with.
The abuse of greatness is when it disjoins
Remorse from power; and, to speak truth of Cæsar,
I have not known when his affections sway'd   20
More than his reason. But 'tis a common proof,
That lowliness is young ambition's ladder,
Whereto the climber-upward turns his face;
But when he once attains the upmost round,   24
He then unto the ladder turns his back,
Looks in the clouds, scorning the base degrees
By which he did ascend. So Cæsar may:
Then, lest he may, prevent. And, since the quarrel 28
Will bear no colour for the thing he is,
Fashion it thus; that what he is, augmented,
Would run to these and these extremities;
And therefore think him as a serpent's egg   32
Which hatch'd, would, as his kind, grow mischievous,
And kill him in the shell.

Enter Lucius.

Luc. The taper burneth in your closet, sir.
Searching the window for a flint, I found   36
This paper, thus seal'd up; and I am sure
It did not lie there when I went to bed.

Bru. Get you to bed again; it is not day.
Is not to-morrow, boy, the ides of March?   40
Luc. I know not, sir.
Bru. Look in the calendar, and bring me word.

---

15 Crown him that; *cf. n.*   19 Remorse: *mercy, conscience*
20 affections: *passions*   21 proof: *proved experience*
26 degrees: *steps, rungs*
28 prevent: *be beforehand*   quarrel: *attack on him, accusation*
29 colour: *justification*   30 Fashion: *put, formulate*
31 these and these: *such and such*
33 as his kind: *as is the nature of his species*   35 closet: *study*

   Luc. I will, sir.   *Exit.*
   Bru. The exhalations whizzing in the air   44
Give so much light that I may read by them.
                  Opens the letter, and reads.
'Brutus, thou sleep'st: awake, and see thyself.
Shall Rome, &c. Speak, strike, redress!
Brutus, thou sleep'st: awake!'   48
Such instigations have been often dropp'd
Where I have took them up.
'Shall Rome, &c.' Thus must I piece it out:
Shall Rome stand under one man's awe? What,
    Rome?   52
My ancestors did from the streets of Rome
The Tarquin drive, when he was call'd a king.
'Speak, strike, redress!' Am I entreated
To speak, and strike? O Rome, I make thee
    promise: 56
If the redress will follow, thou receivest
Thy full petition at the hand of Brutus!

              Enter Lucius.

   Luc. Sir, March is wasted fourteen days.   59
                  Knocking within.
   Bru. 'Tis good. Go to the gate: somebody knocks.
                [Exit Lucius.]
Since Cassius first did whet me against Cæsar,
I have not slept.
Between the acting of a dreadful thing
And the first motion, all the interim is   64
Like a phantasma, or a hideous dream:
The genius and the mortal instruments

---

44 exhalations: *meteors*
58 Thy full petition: *full measure of what thou askest*
59 fourteen; *cf. n.*   61, 62 *Cf. n.*   64 motion: *instigation, inception*
65 phantasma: *vision, phantasmagoria*
66 genius: *the guardian spirit, within man*   mortal instruments: *human faculties*

Are then in council; and the state of man,
Like to a little kingdom, suffers then   68
The nature of an insurrection.

Enter Lucius.

Luc. Sir, 'tis your brother Cassius at the door,
Who doth desire to see you.
   Bru.   Is he alone?
   Luc. No, sir, there are moe with him.
   Bru.   Do you know them?   72
   Luc. No, sir; their hats are pluck'd about their
     ears,
And half their faces buried in their cloaks,
That by no means I may discover them
By any mark of favour.
   Bru.   Let 'em enter.   76
                         [Exit Lucius.]
They are the faction. O conspiracy,
Sham'st thou to show thy dangerous brow by night,
When evils are most free? O then by day
Where wilt thou find a cavern dark enough   80
To mask thy monstrous visage? Seek none, con-
     spiracy;
Hide it in smiles and affability:
For if thou path, thy native semblance on,
Not Erebus itself were dim enough   84
To hide thee from prevention.

*Enter the Conspirators, Cassius, Casca, Decius,
    Cinna, Metellus, and Trebonius.*

70 brother: *he had married Brutus' sister, Junia*
72 moe: *more, others*
76 mark of favour: *trait of countenance*
77 faction: *band of conspirators*
83 path: *walk, proceed*   native: *natural*   on: *being on*
84 Erebus: *gloomy region leading to Hades (the name signifies
   'darkness')*   85 prevention: *being forestalled*

Cas. I think we are too bold upon your rest:
Good morrow, Brutus; do we trouble you?

Bru. I have been up this hour, awake all night.   88
Know I these men that come along with you?

Cas. Yes, every man of them; and no man here
But honours you; and every one doth wish
You had but that opinion of yourself   92
Which every noble Roman bears of you.
This is Trebonius.

Bru.   He is welcome hither.

Cas. This, Decius Brutus.

Bru.   He is welcome too.

Cas. This, Casca; this, Cinna;   96
And this, Metellus Cimber.

Bru.   They are all welcome.
What watchful cares do interpose themselves
Betwixt your eyes and night?

Cas. Shall I entreat a word?   100

               [*Brutus and Cassius*] *whisper.*

Dec. Here lies the east: doth not the day break
   here?

Casca. No.

Cin. O pardon, sir, it doth; and yon grey lines
That fret the clouds are messengers of day.   104

Casca. You shall confess that you are both
   deceiv'd.
Here, as I point my sword, the sun arises;
Which is a great way growing on the south,
Weighing the youthful season of the year.   108
Some two months hence up higher toward the north
He first presents his fire; and the high east
Stands, as the Capitol, directly here.

---

86 bold: *i.e., in intruding*   90 and no: *and there is no*
104 fret: *chequer*   106 as: *where*
107 growing on: *tending toward*   108 Weighing: *on account of*

Bru. Give me your hands all over, one by one.   112
Cas. And let us swear our resolution.
Bru. No, not an oath: if not the face of men,
The sufferance of our souls, the time's abuse,—
If these be motives weak, break off betimes,   116
And every man hence to his idle bed;
So let high-sighted tyranny range on,
Till each man drop by lottery. But if these,
As I am sure they do, bear fire enough   120
To kindle cowards and to steel with valour
The melting spirits of women, then, countrymen,
What need we any spur but our own cause
To prick us to redress? what other bond   124
Than secret Romans, that have spoke the word
And will not palter? and what other oath
Than honesty to honesty engag'd,
That this shall be, or we will fall for it?   128
Swear priests and cowards and men cautelous,
Old feeble carrions and such suffering souls
That welcome wrongs: unto bad causes swear
Such creatures as men doubt; but do not stain   132
The even virtue of our enterprise,
Nor th' insuppressive mettle of our spirits,
To think that or our cause or our performance
Did need an oath; when every drop of blood   136
That every Roman bears, and nobly bears,
Is guilty of a several bastardy,
If he do break the smallest particle

112 all over: *successively*
114 face of men: *mute appeal in the people's looks*
115 sufferance: *suffering, distress*   the . . . abuse: *abuses of the time*
                                               116 betimes: *before it's too late*
118 high-sighted: *haughty*   119 lottery: *arbitrary decree*
123 What: *why*   125 Than secret: *than that of resolute*
126 palter: *play fast and loose*   129 cautelous: *crafty, deceitful*
130 carrions: *wretches no better than soulless carcasses*   suffering: *long-suffering*   133 even: *just*
134 insuppressive: *irrepressible*   135 or . . . or: *either . . . or*
138 *Is individually condemned as illegitimate*

Of any promise that hath pass'd from him.   140
  Cas. But what of Cicero? Shall we sound him?
I think he will stand very strong with us.
  Casca. Let us not leave him out.
  Cin.   No, by no means.
  Met. O let us have him; for his silver hairs
Will purchase us a good opinion   145
And buy men's voices to commend our deeds:
It shall be said his judgment rul'd our hands;
Our youths and wildness shall no whit appear,
But all be buried in his gravity.   149
  Bru. O name him not: let us not break with him;
For he will never follow anything
That other men begin.
  Cas.   Then leave him out. 152
  Casca. Indeed he is not fit.
  Dec. Shall no man else be touch'd but only Cæsar?
  Cas. Decius, well urg'd. I think it is not meet,
Mark Antony, so well belov'd of Cæsar,   156
Should outlive Cæsar: we shall find of him
A shrewd contriver; and you know, his means,
If he improve them, may well stretch so far
As to annoy us all; which to prevent,   160
Let Antony and Cæsar fall together.
  Bru. Our course will seem too bloody, Caius Cas-
    sius,
To cut the head off and then hack the limbs,
Like wrath in death and envy afterwards;   164
For Antony is but a limb of Cæsar.
Let us be sacrificers, but not butchers, Caius.
We all stand up against the spirit of Cæsar;

150 break with: *broach our plan to*   157 of: *in*
158 shrewd contriver: *malevolent plotter*
159 improve: *make the most of*
160 annoy: *seriously injure*
164 envy: *vindictiveness*

And in the spirit of men there is no blood: 168
O then that we could come by Cæsar's spirit,
And not dismember Cæsar! But, alas,
Cæsar must bleed for it. And, gentle friends,
Let's kill him boldly, but not wrathfully; 172
Let's carve him as a dish fit for the gods,
Not hew him as a carcass fit for hounds:
And let our hearts, as subtle masters do,
Stir up their servants to an act of rage, 176
And after seem to chide 'em. This shall make
Our purpose necessary and not envious;
Which so appearing to the common eyes,
We shall be call'd purgers, not murderers. 180
And, for Mark Antony, think not of him;
For he can do no more than Cæsar's arm
When Cæsar's head is off.

  Cas.   Yet I fear him;
For in the ingrafted love he bears to Cæsar— 184
  Bru. Alas, good Cassius, do not think of him.
If he love Cæsar, all that he can do
Is to himself: take thought, and die for Cæsar.
And that were much he should, for he is given
To sports, to wildness, and much company. 189
  Treb. There is no fear in him; let him not die;
For he will live, and laugh at this hereafter.

              Clock strikes.

  Bru. Peace! count the clock.
  Cas.   The clock hath stricken three. 192
  Treb. 'Tis time to part.
  Cas.   But it is doubtful yet
Whether Cæsar will come forth to-day or no;

---

184 ingrafted: *deeply rooted*
187 Is to: *concerns, affects, only* take thought: *despond*
188 that . . . should: *even that would be more than might be expected*
190 fear: *cause for fear*

For he is superstitious grown of late,
Quite from the main opinion he held once   196
Of fantasy, of dreams, and ceremonies.
It may be, these apparent prodigies,
The unaccustom'd terror of this night,
And the persuasion of his augurers,   200
May hold him from the Capitol to-day.

 Dec. Never fear that: if he be so resolv'd,
I can o'ersway him; for he loves to hear
That unicorns may be betray'd with trees,   204
And bears with glasses, elephants with holes,
Lions with toils, and men with flatterers;
But when I tell him he hates flatterers,
He says he does, being then most flattered.   208
Let me work;
For I can give his humour the true bent,
And I will bring him to the Capitol.

 Cas. Nay, we will all of us be there to fetch
  him.   212

 Bru. By the eighth hour: is that the uttermost.

 Cin. Be that the uttermost, and fail not then.

 Met. Caius Ligarius doth bear Cæsar hard,
Who rated him for speaking well of Pompey: 216
I wonder none of you have thought of him.

 Bru. Now, good Metellus, go along by him:
He loves me well, and I have given him reasons;
Send him but hither, and I'll fashion him.   220

 Cas. The morning comes upon 's: we'll leave you,
  Brutus.
And, friends, disperse yourselves; but all remember

---

196 from . . . main: *changed from the general*
198 apparent: *manifest*
204 trees: *by luring them to drive their horns too firmly into trees*
205 glasses: *mirrors, to distract their attention* holes: *pitfalls*
206 toils: *nets, snares* 210 humour: *disposition; cf. n. on line 250*
213 uttermost: *latest*   216 rated: *berated, reprimanded*
218 by him: *by his house* 220 fashion: *like modern 'whip into shape'*

What you have said, and show yourselves true
    Romans.
   Bru. Good gentlemen, look fresh and merrily;   224
Let not our looks put on our purposes,
But bear it as our Roman actors do,
With untir'd spirits and formal constancy:
And so good morrow to you every one.   228
                     Exeunt.   Manet Brutus.
Boy! Lucius! Fast asleep? It is no matter;
Enjoy the honey-heavy dew of slumber:
Thou hast no figures nor no fantasies
Which busy care draws in the brains of men;
Therefore thou sleep'st so sound.   233

             Enter Portia.

   Por.   Brutus, my lord!
   Bru. Portia, what mean you? Wherefore rise you
    now?
It is not for your health thus to commit
Your weak condition to the raw cold morning.   236
   Por. Nor for yours neither. You've ungently,
    Brutus,
Stole from my bed; and yesternight at supper
You suddenly arose, and walk'd about,
Musing and sighing, with your arms across,   240
And when I ask'd you what the matter was,
You star'd upon me with ungentle looks.
I urg'd you further; then you scratch'd your head,
And too impatiently stamp'd with your foot;   244
Yet I insisted, yet you answer'd not,
But with an angry wafture of your hand
Gave sign for me to leave you. So I did,
Fearing to strengthen that impatience   248

227 formal constancy: *dignified self-possession*
231 figures: *pictures created by imagination*

Which seem'd too much enkindled, and withal
Hoping it was but an effect of humour,
Which sometime hath his hour with every man.
It will not let you eat, nor talk, nor sleep,   252
And could it work so much upon your shape
As it hath much prevail'd on your condition,
I should not know you, Brutus. Dear my lord,
Make me acquainted with your cause of grief.   256

 Bru. I am not well in health, and that is all.

 Por. Brutus is wise, and were he not in health,
He would embrace the means to come by it.

 Bru. Why, so I do. Good Portia, go to bed.   260

 Por. Is Brutus sick, and is it physical
To walk unbraced and suck up the humours
Of the dank morning? What! is Brutus sick,
And will he steal out of his wholesome bed   264
To dare the vile contagion of the night,
And tempt the rheumy and unpurged air
To add unto his sickness? No, my Brutus;
You have some sick offence within your mind,   268
Which, by the right and virtue of my place,
I ought to know of; and, upon my knees,
I charm you, by my once-commended beauty,
By all your vows of love, and that great vow   272
Which did incorporate and make us one,
That you unfold to me, your self, your half,
Why you are heavy, and what men to-night
Have had resort to you; for here have been   276
Some six or seven, who did hide their faces
Even from darkness.

 Bru.   **Kneel not, gentle Portia.**

250 humour; *cf. n.* 253, 254 *(outward)* shape, *(inward)* condition
261 physical: *healthful*
266 rheumy: *causing rheumatic diseases* unpurged: *unpurified by*
 the sun   268 sick offence: *unhealthy trouble*
271 charm: *conjure, entreat*

Por. I should not need, if you were gentle Brutus.
Within the bond of marriage, tell me, Brutus,   280
Is it excepted I should know no secrets
That appertain to you? Am I yourself
But, as it were, in sort or limitation,
To keep with you at meals, comfort your bed,   284
And talk to you sometimes? Dwell I but in the
     suburbs
Of your good pleasure? If it be no more,
Portia is Brutus' harlot, not his wife.

Bru. You are my true and honourable wife,   288
As dear to me as are the ruddy drops
That visit my sad heart.

Por. If this were true then should I know this
     secret.
I grant I am a woman, but, withal,   292
A woman that Lord Brutus took to wife;
I grant I am a woman, but, withal,
A woman well-reputed, Cato's daughter.
Think you I am no stronger than my sex,   296
Being so father'd and so husbanded?
Tell me your counsels, I will not disclose 'em.
I have made strong proof of my constancy,
Giving myself a voluntary wound,   300
Here, in the thigh: can I bear that with patience
And not my husband's secrets?

Bru.   O ye gods,
Render me worthy of this noble wife!

                              Knock [*within*].
Hark, hark! one knocks. Portia, go in awhile;   304
And by and by thy bosom shall partake
The secrets of my heart.

283 in . . . limitation: *only after a fashion or with restrictions*
292 withal: *with this saving reservation*
295 Cato: *Marcus Porcius Cato, 'of Utica'*

All my engagements I will construe to thee,
All the charactery of my sad brows.   308
Leave me with haste.   *Exit Portia.*

Lucius, who's that knocks?

Enter Lucius and Ligarius.

Luc. Here is a sick man that would speak with you.
Bru. Caius Ligarius, that Metellus spoke of.
Boy, stand aside.   Caius Ligarius! how?   312
   Lig. Vouchsafe good morrow from a feeble tongue.
   Bru. O what a time have you chose out, brave
      Caius,
To wear a kerchief!   Would you were not sick!
   Lig. I am not sick if Brutus have in hand
Any exploit worthy the name of honour.   317
   Bru. Such an exploit have I in hand, Ligarius,
Had you a healthful ear to hear of it.
   Lig. By all the gods that Romans bow before,
I here discard my sickness!   Soul of Rome,   321
Brave son, deriv'd from honourable loins,
Thou, like an exorcist, hast conjur'd up
My mortified spirit.   Now bid me run,
And I will strive with things impossible;   325
Yea, get the better of them.   What's to do?
   Bru. A piece of work that will make sick men
      whole.
   Lig. But are not some whole that we must make
      sick?   328
   Bru. That must we also.   What it is, my Caius,
I shall unfold to thee as we are going
To whom it must be done.

307 engagements: *undertakings that I stand committed to*   construe:
   explain   308 charactery: *writing, message*
309 who's: *who is it*   313 Vouchsafe: *vouchsafe to receive*
315 kerchief: *swathing for the head of the sick*
323 exorcist: *magician*   324 mortified: *deadened*
331 To whom: *to him to whom*

 Lig.   Set on your foot,
And with a heart new-fir'd I follow you,   332
To do I know not what; but it sufficeth
That Brutus leads me on.   *Thunder.*
 Bru.   Follow me then.
            Exeunt.

Scene Two

[*Cæsar's House*]

*Thunder and lightning. Enter Julius Cæsar in his
night-gown.*

 Cæs. Nor heaven nor earth have been at peace to-
  night:
Thrice hath Calpurnia in her sleep cried out,
'Help, ho! They murder Cæsar!' Who's within?

     Enter a Servant.

 Serv. My lord!   4
 Cæs. Go bid the priests do present sacrifice,
And bring me their opinions of success.
 Serv. I will, my lord.   *Exit.*

     Enter Calpurnia.

 Cal. What mean you, Cæsar? Think you to walk
  forth?   8
You shall not stir out of your house to-day.
 Cæs. Cæsar shall forth: the things that threaten'd
  me
Ne'er look'd but on my back; when they shall see
The face of Cæsar, they are vanished.   12
 Cal. Cæsar, I never stood on ceremonies,

Scene Two S. d. night-gown: *dressing-gown*
5 present: *immediate*   6 success: *the future*
13 stood on ceremonies: *laid stress on omens*

Yet now they fright me. There is one within,
Besides the things that we have heard and seen,
Recounts most horrid sights seen by the watch.
A lioness hath whelped in the streets;   17
And graves have yawn'd and yielded up their dead;
Fierce fiery warriors fought upon the clouds,
In ranks and squadrons and right form of war,
Which drizzled blood upon the Capitol;   21
The noise of battle hurtled in the air,
Horses did neigh, and dying men did groan,
And ghosts did shriek and squeal about the streets. 24
O Cæsar, these things are beyond all use,
And I do fear them.

    Cæs.   What can be avoided
Whose end is purpos'd by the mighty gods?
Yet Cæsar shall go forth; for these predictions   28
Are to the world in general as to Cæsar.

    Cal. When beggars die there are no comets seen;
The heavens themselves blaze forth the death of
        princes.

    Cæs. Cowards die many times before their
        deaths;   32
The valiant never taste of death but once.
Of all the wonders that I yet have heard,
It seems to me most strange that men should fear;
Seeing that death, a necessary end,   36
Will come when it will come.

                        Enter a Servant.

                            What say the augurers?
    Serv. They would not have you to stir forth to-day.
Plucking the entrails of an offering forth,

20 right form: *regular formations*
22 hurtled: *emitted sounds of conflict, clashed*
25 use: *previous experience*
27 end: *accomplishment*   29 Are to: *are as applicable to*

They could not find a heart within the beast.   40

Cæs. The gods do this in shame of cowardice:
Cæsar should be a beast without a heart
If he should stay at home to-day for fear.
No, Cæsar shall not; danger knows full well   44
That Cæsar is more dangerous than he:
We are two lions litter'd in one day,
And I the elder and more terrible:
And Cæsar shall go forth.

Cal.   Alas, my lord,   48
Your wisdom is consum'd in confidence.
Do not go forth to-day: call it my fear
That keeps you in the house, and not your own.
We'll send Mark Antony to the senate-house,   52
And he shall say you are not well to-day:
Let me, upon my knee, prevail in this.

Cæs. Mark Antony shall say I am not well;
And, for thy humour, I will stay at home.   56

Enter Decius.

Here's Decius Brutus, he shall tell them so.

Dec. Cæsar, all hail! Good morrow, worthy Cæsar:
I come to fetch you to the senate-house.

Cæs. And you are come in very happy time   60
To bear my greeting to the senators,
And tell them that I will not come to-day:
Cannot, is false, and that I dare not, falser;
I will not come to-day: tell them so, Decius.   64

Cal. Say he is sick.

Cæs.   Shall Cæsar send a lie?
Have I in conquest stretch'd mine arm so far
To be afeard to tell greybeards the truth?
Decius, go tell them Cæsar will not come.   68

49 confidence: *over-confidence*   56 humour: *whim, caprice*

Dec. Most mighty Cæsar, let me know some cause,
Lest I be laugh'd at when I tell them so.

Cæs. The cause is in my will: I will not come;
That is enough to satisfy the senate: 72
But for your private satisfaction,
Because I love you, I will let you know:
Calpurnia here, my wife, stays me at home:
She dreamt to-night she saw my statue,   76
Which, like a fountain with a hundred spouts,
Did run pure blood; and many lusty Romans
Came smiling, and did bathe their hands in it:
And these does she apply for warnings and por-
          tents,   80
And evils imminent; and on her knee
Hath begg'd that I will stay at home to-day.

Dec. This dream is all amiss interpreted;
It was a vision fair and fortunate: 34
Your statue spouting blood in many pipes,
In which so many smiling Romans bath'd,
Signifies that from you great Rome shall suck
Reviving blood, and that great men shall press
For tinctures, stains, relics, and cognizance.   89
This by Calpurnia's dream is signified.

Cæs. And this way have you well expounded it.

Dec. I have, when you have heard what I can
          say;   92
And know it now: the senate have concluded
To give this day a crown to mighty Cæsar.
If you shall send them word you will not come,
Their minds may change.   Besides, it were a mock 96
Apt to be render'd, for some one to say,

---

75 stays: *keeps*   88 press: *crowd about*
89 tinctures: *healing medicines; cf. n.*   stains: *assimilable traces*
    (tinges) of Cæsar's qualities   relics: *i.e., religious benefits*   cog-
    nizance: *heraldic emblems, i.e., social benefits*
96 mock: *gibe*

'Break up the senate till another time,
When Cæsar's wife shall meet with better dreams.'
If Cæsar hide himself, shall they not whisper,   100
'Lo, Cæsar is afraid'?
Pardon me, Cæsar; for my dear dear love
To your proceeding bids me tell you this,
And reason to my love is liable.   104
   Cæs. How foolish do your fears seem now, Cal-
    purnia!
I am ashamed I did yield to them.
Give me my robe, for I will go.

Enter Brutus, Ligarius, Metellus, Casca, Trebonius,
Cinna, and Publius.

And look where Publius is come to fetch me.   108
   Pub. Good morrow, Cæsar.
   Cæs.   Welcome, Publius.
What, Brutus, are you stirr'd so early too?
Good morrow, Casca. Caius Ligarius,
Cæsar was ne'er so much your enemy   112
As that same ague which hath made you lean.
What is 't o'clock?
   Bru.   Cæsar, 'tis strucken eight.
   Cæs. I thank you for your pains and courtesy.

Enter Antony.

See, Antony, that revels long o' nights,   116
Is notwithstanding up. Good morrow, Antony.
   Ant. So to most noble Cæsar.
   Cæs.   Bid them prepare within:
I am to blame to be thus waited for.
Now, Cinna; now, Metellus; what, Trebonius,
I have an hour's talk in store for you;   121
Remember that you call on me to-day:

103 proceeding: *career*   104 liable: *subservient*

Be near me, that I may remember you.

   Treb. Cæsar, I will:—[*Aside.*] and so near will I
   be,   124

That your best friends shall wish I had been further.

   Cæs. Good friends, go in, and taste some wine with
   me;

And we, like friends, will straightway go together.

   Bru. [*Aside.*] That every 'like' is not 'the same,'
   O Cæsar,   128

The heart of Brutus yearns to think upon.   *Exeunt.*

Scene Three

[*A Street near the Capitol*]

Enter Artemidorus [reading a paper].

   Art. 'Cæsar, beware of Brutus; take heed of
Cassius; come not near Casca; have an eye to
Cinna; trust not Trebonius; mark well Metellus Cimber; Decius Brutus loves thee not; thou
hast wronged Caius Ligarius. There is but one
mind in all these men, and it is bent against
Cæsar. If thou beest not immortal, look about
you: security gives way to conspiracy. The
mighty gods defend thee! Thy lover,   9

                         ARTEMIDORUS.'

Here will I stand till Cæsar pass along,
And as a suitor will I give him this.   12
My heart laments that virtue cannot live
Out of the teeth of emulation.
If thou read this, O Cæsar, thou mayest live;
If not, the Fates with traitors do contrive.   *Exit.*

128 *Cf. n.*   129 yearns: *grieves*
8 security gives way: *unguardedness yields opportunity*
9 lover: *friend*
14 Out . . . teeth: *free from the bite*   emulation: *grudging jealousy*

Scene Four

[Another part of the same Street, before the house of Brutus]

Enter Portia and Lucius.

Por. I prithee, boy, run to the senate-house;
Stay not to answer me, but get thee gone.
Why dost thou stay?
  Luc.   To know my errand, madam.
Por. I would have had thee there, and here
  again,   4
Ere I can tell thee what thou shouldst do there.
O constancy, be strong upon my side;
Set a huge mountain 'tween my heart and tongue;
I have a man's mind, but a woman's might. 8
How hard it is for women to keep counsel!
Art thou here yet?
  Luc.   Madam, what shall I do?
Run to the Capitol, and nothing else?
And so return to you, and nothing else? 12
 Por. Yes, bring me word, boy, if thy lord look well,
For he went sickly forth; and take good note
What Cæsar doth, what suitors press to him.
Hark, boy! what noise is that?   16
  Luc. I hear none, madam.
  Por.   Prithee, listen well:
I heard a bustling rumour, like a fray,
And the wind brings it from the Capitol.
  Luc. Sooth, madam, I hear nothing. 20

Enter the Soothsayer.

 Por. Come hither, fellow: which way hast thou
  been?

20 Sooth: *in truth*

Sooth. At mine own house, good lady.

Por. What is 't o'clock?

Sooth. About the ninth hour, lady.

Por. Is Cæsar yet gone to the Capitol? 24

Sooth. Madam, not yet: I go to take my stand,
To see him pass on to the Capitol.

Por. Thou hast some suit to Cæsar, hast thou not?

Sooth. That I have, lady: if it will please Cæ-
sar 28
To be so good to Cæsar as to hear me,
I shall beseech him to befriend himself.

Por. Why, know'st thou any harm's intended
towards him?

Sooth. None that I know will be, much that I fear
may chance. 32
Good morrow to you. Here the street is narrow:
The throng that follows Cæsar at the heels,
Of senators, of prætors, common suitors,
Will crowd a feeble man almost to death: 36
I'll get me to a place more void, and there
Speak to great Cæsar as he comes along. *Exit.*

Por. I must go in. Ay me! how weak a thing
The heart of woman is. O Brutus, 40
The heavens speed thee in thine enterprise!
Sure, the boy heard me.—Brutus hath a suit
That Cæsar will not grant.—O, I grow faint.—
Run, Lucius, and commend me to my lord; 44
Say I am merry: come to me again,
And bring me word what he doth say to thee.

Exeunt.

37 void: *open*

ACT THIRD

Scene One

[Before the Capitol]

Flourish. Enter Cæsar, Brutus, Cassius, Casca, De-
cius, Metellus, Trebonius, Cinna, Antony, Lepi-
dus, Artemidorus, [Popilius,] Publius, the Sooth-
sayer [and Others].

Cæs. *[To the Soothsayer.]* The ides of March are
come.

Sooth. Ay, Cæsar; but not gone.

Art. Hail, Cæsar! Read this schedule.

Dec. Trebonius doth desire you to o'er-read,   4
At your best leisure, this his humble suit.

Art. O Cæsar, read mine first; for mine's a suit
That touches Cæsar nearer. Read it, great Cæsar.

Cæs. What touches us ourself shall be last
serv'd.   8

Art. Delay not, Cæsar; read it instantly.

Cæs. What, is the fellow mad?

Pub.   Sirrah, give place.

Cæs. What, urge you your petitions in the street?
Come to the Capitol.   12

[Cæsar goes up to the Senate-House, the rest
following.]

Pop. I wish your enterprise to-day may thrive.

Cas. What enterprise, Popilius?

Pop.   Fare you well.

                   [Advances to Cæsar.]

Bru. What said Popilius Lena?

Cas. He wish'd to-day our enterprise might
   thrive.   16
I fear our purpose is discovered.

Bru. Look, how he makes to Cæsar: mark him.

Cas. Casca, be sudden, for we fear prevention.
Brutus, what shall be done? If this be known,   20
Cassius or Cæsar never shall turn back,
For I will slay myself.

Bru.   Cassius, be constant:
Popilius Lena speaks not of our purposes;
For, look, he smiles, and Cæsar doth not change.   24

Cas. Trebonius knows his time; for, look you,
   Brutus,
He draws Mark Antony out of the way.

                     [Exeunt Antony and Trebonius.]

Dec. Where is Metellus Cimber? Let him go,
And presently prefer his suit to Cæsar.   28

Bru. He is address'd; press near and second him.

Cin. Casca, you are the first that rears your hand.

Cæs. Are we all ready? What is now amiss,
That Cæsar and his senate must redress?   32

Met. Most high, most mighty, and most puissant
   Cæsar,
Metellus Cimber throws before thy seat
A humble heart,—   *[Kneeling.]*

Cæs.   I must prevent thee, Cimber.
These couchings and these lowly courtesies,   36
Might fire the blood of ordinary men,
And turn pre-ordinance and first decree
Into the law of children. Be not fond,

22 constant: *unmoved*
28 prefer: *present, offer*
29 address'd: *ready*
36 couchings: *prostrations*   courtesies: *bowings*
38 pre-ordinance: *what is already ordained*
39 law of children: *arbitrary uncertainty*   fond: *foolish*

To think that Cæsar bears such rebel blood   40
That will be thaw'd from the true quality
With that which melteth fools; I mean sweet words,
Low-crooked curtsies, and base spaniel fawning.
Thy brother by decree is banished: 44
If thou dost bend and pray and fawn for him,
I spurn thee like a cur out of my way.
Know, Cæsar doth not wrong, nor without cause
Will he be satisfied.   48

    Met. Is there no voice more worthy than my own,
To sound more sweetly in great Cæsar's ear
For the repealing of my banish'd brother?

    Bru. I kiss thy hand, but not in flattery, Cæsar;   52
Desiring thee, that Publius Cimber may
Have an immediate freedom of repeal.

    Cæs. What, Brutus!

    Cas.   Pardon, Cæsar; Cæsar, pardon:
As low as to thy foot doth Cassius fall,   56
To beg enfranchisement for Publius Cimber.

    Cæs. I could be well mov'd if I were as you;
If I could pray to move, prayers would move me:
But I am constant as the northern star,   60
Of whose true-fix'd and resting quality
There is no fellow in the firmament.
The skies are painted with unnumber'd sparks,
They are all fire and every one doth shine,   64
But there's but one in all doth hold his place:
So, in the world; 'tis furnish'd well with men,
And men are flesh and blood, and apprehensive;
Yet in the number I do know but one   68

40 rebel: *ungovernable*   42 With: *by*
43 Low-crooked: *low-bending*   curtsies: *same as 'courtesies,' line 36*
    spaniel: *servile, obsequious*   47, 48 *Cf. n.*
51 repealing: *recalling*
54 freedom of repeal: *free, unconditional recall*   59 *Cf. n.*
61 resting: *stationary*   63 painted: *decorated*
67 apprehensive: *intelligent*

That unassailable holds on his rank,
Unshak'd of motion: and that I am he
Let me a little show it, even in this,
That I was constant Cimber should be banish'd,
And constant do remain to keep him so.   73

  Cin. O Cæsar,—

  Cæs.   Hence! Wilt thou lift up Olympus?

  Dec. Great Cæsar,—

  Cæs.   Doth not Brutus bootless kneel?

  Casca. Speak, hands, for me!   76

                    They stab Cæsar.

  Cæs. Et tu, Brute? Then fall, Cæsar!   *Dies.*

  Cin. Liberty! Freedom! Tyranny is dead!
Run hence, proclaim, cry it about the streets.

  Cas. Some to the common pulpits, and cry out,   80
'Liberty, freedom, and enfranchisement!'

  Bru. People and senators, be not affrighted;
Fly not; stand still; ambition's debt is paid.

    [*Exeunt all but the Conspirators and Publius.*]

  Casca. Go to the pulpit, Brutus.

  Dec.   And Cassius too.   84

  Bru. Where's Publius?

  Cin. Here, quite confounded with this mutiny.

  Met. Stand fast together, lest some friend of Cæ-
    sar's
Should chance—   88

  Bru. Talk not of standing. Publius, good cheer;
There is no harm intended to your person,
Nor to no Roman else; so tell them, Publius.

  Cas. And leave us, Publius; lest that the people,   92
Rushing on us, should do your age some mischief.

69 holds on: *maintains*   rank: *position*
75 bootless: *unavailingly*
80 common pulpits: *public rostra*
89 good cheer: *be of good cheer, undismayed*

Bru. Do so; and let no man abide this deed
But we the doers.   [*Exit Publius.*]

Enter Trebonius.

Cas. Where is Antony?
Tre.   Fled to his house amaz'd.   96
Men, wives, and children stare, cry out, and run,
As it were doomsday.
Bru.   Fates, we will know your pleasures.
That we shall die, we know; 'tis but the time
And drawing days out, that men stand upon.   100
Casca. Why, he that cuts off twenty years of life
Cuts off so many years of fearing death.
Bru. Grant that, and then is death a benefit:
So are we Cæsar's friends, that have abridg'd   104
His time of fearing death. Stoop, Romans, stoop,
And let us bathe our hands in Cæsar's blood
Up to the elbows, and besmear our swords:
Then walk we forth, even to the market-place;   108
And waving our red weapons o'er our heads,
Let's all cry, 'Peace, freedom, and liberty!'
Cas. Stoop, then, and wash. How many ages hence
Shall this our lofty scene be acted over,   112
In states unborn and accents yet unknown!
Bru. How many times shall Cæsar bleed in sport,
That now on Pompey's basis lies along,
No worthier than the dust!
Cas.   So oft as that shall be,   116
So often shall the knot of us be call'd
The men that gave their country liberty.
Dec. What, shall we forth?
Cas.   Ay, every man away:

94 abide: *pay the penalty for*   97 wives: *women*
100 drawing . . . out: *prolonging their life*   stand upon: *lay stress
on, worry about*
115 Pompey's basis: *pedestal of Pompey's statue*   along: *outstretched*
117 knot: *group*

Brutus shall lead; and we will grace his heels
With the most boldest and best hearts of Rome. 121

Enter a Servant.

Bru. Soft, who comes here? A friend of Antony's.
Serv. Thus, Brutus, did my master bid me kneel;
Thus did Mark Antony bid me fall down; 124
And, being prostrate, thus he bade me say:
Brutus is noble, wise, valiant, and honest;
Cæsar was mighty, bold, royal, and loving:
Say I love Brutus, and I honour him; 128
Say I fear'd Cæsar, honour'd him, and lov'd him.
If Brutus will vouchsafe that Antony
May safely come to him, and be resolv'd
How Cæsar hath deserv'd to lie in death, 132
Mark Antony shall not love Cæsar dead
So well as Brutus living; but will follow
The fortunes and affairs of noble Brutus
Thorough the hazards of this untrod state 136
With all true faith. So says my master Antony.
Bru. Thy master is a wise and valiant Roman;
I never thought him worse.
Tell him, so please him come unto this place,
He shall be satisfied; and, by my honour, 141
Depart untouch'd.
    Serv.   I'll fetch him presently.

                              Exit Servant.

Bru. I know that we shall have him well to friend.
Cas. I wish we may: but yet have I a mind
That fears him much; and my misgiving still
Falls shrewdly to the purpose. 146

131 resolv'd: *convinced, satisfied*
136 Thorough: *throughout*   untrod: *novel, precarious*
140 so please him: *if he is willing to*
143 well to friend: *as a good friend*
145, 146 still . . . purpose: *always proves only too well grounded*

Enter Antony.

Bru. But here comes Antony.   Welcome, Mark
   Antony.

Ant. O mighty Cæsar! dost thou lie so low?
Are all thy conquests, glories, triumphs, spoils,
Shrunk to this little measure?   Fare thee well.
I know not, gentlemen, what you intend,   151
Who else must be let blood, who else is rank:
If I myself, there is no hour so fit
As Cæsar's death's hour, nor no instrument
Of half that worth as those your swords, made rich
With the most noble blood of all this world.   156
I do beseech ye, if ye bear me hard,
Now, whilst your purpled hands do reek and smoke,
Fulfil your pleasure.   Live a thousand years,
I shall not find myself so apt to die: 160
No place will please me so, no mean of death,
As here by Cæsar, and by you cut off,
The choice and master spirits of this age.

Bru. O Antony! beg not your death of us.
Though now we must appear bloody and cruel,   165
As, by our hands and this our present act,
You see we do, yet see you but our hands
And this the bleeding business they have done:
Our hearts you see not; they are pitiful;   169
And pity to the general wrong of Rome—
As fire drives out fire, so pity pity—
Hath done this deed on Cæsar.   For your part,
To you our swords have leaden points, Mark An-
   tony: 173
Our arms in strength of malice, and our hearts

---

152 let blood: *bled, for medical purposes*   rank: *diseased from sur-*
   feiting   159 Live: *if I live*   feiting
161 mean: *means*   160 apt: *ready, fit*
174 malice: *power (but not wish) to harm; cf. n.* 162 by Cæsar: *beside Cæsar*

Of brothers' temper, do receive you in
With all kind love, good thoughts, and reverence.   176
   Cas. Your voice shall be as strong as any man's
In the disposing of new dignities.
   Bru. Only be patient till we have appeas'd
The multitude, beside themselves with fear,   180
And then we will deliver you the cause
Why I, that did love Cæsar when I struck him,
Have thus proceeded.
   Ant.   I doubt not of your wisdom.
Let each man render me his bloody hand: 184
First, Marcus Brutus, will I shake with you;
Next, Caius Cassius, do I take your hand;
Now, Decius Brutus, yours; now yours, Metellus;
Yours, Cinna; and, my valiant Casca, yours;   188
Though last, not least in love, yours, good Trebonius.
Gentlemen all,—alas! what shall I say?
My credit now stands on such slippery ground,
That one of two bad ways you must conceit me,   192
Either a coward or a flatterer.
That I did love thee, Cæsar, O 'tis true:
If then thy spirit look upon us now,
Shall it not grieve thee dearer than thy death,   196
To see thy Antony making his peace,
Shaking the bloody fingers of thy foes,
Most noble, in the presence of thy corse?
Had I as many eyes as thou hast wounds,   200
Weeping as fast as they stream forth thy blood,
It would become me better than to close
In terms of friendship with thine enemies.
Pardon me, Julius. Here wast thou bay'd, brave
     hart;   204

178 disposing . . . dignities: *distributing . . . offices*
199 corse: *corpse*   202 close: *unite*
204 bay'd: *brought to bay*   hart: *stag (an obvious play on words)*

Here didst thou fall; and here thy hunters stand,
Sign'd in thy spoil, and crimson'd in thy lethe.
O world, thou wast the forest to this hart,
And this, indeed, O world, the heart of thee.   208
How like a deer, stricken by many princes,
Dost thou here lie!

    Cas. Mark Antony,—

    Ant.   Pardon me, Caius Cassius:
The enemies of Cæsar shall say this;   212
Then, in a friend, it is cold modesty.

    Cas. I blame you not for praising Cæsar so;
But what compact mean you to have with us?
Will you be prick'd in number of our friends,   216
Or shall we on, and not depend on you?

    Ant. Therefore I took your hands, but was indeed
Sway'd from the point by looking down on Cæsar.
Friends am I with you all, and love you all,   220
Upon this hope, that you shall give me reasons
Why and wherein Cæsar was dangerous.

    Bru. Or else were this a savage spectacle.
Our reasons are so full of good regard   224
That were you, Antony, the son of Cæsar,
You should be satisfied.

    Ant.   That's all I seek:
And am moreover suitor that I may
Produce his body to the market-place,   228
And in the pulpit, as becomes a friend,
Speak in the order of his funeral.

    Bru. You shall, Mark Antony.

    Cas.   Brutus, a word with you.

206 Sign'd . . . spoil: *bearing the bloody mark of thy slaughter*
    lethe: *death (?)*   212 this: *all that he has just been saying*
213 modesty: *moderation*
216 prick'd in number: *marked in the list*
224 good regard: *what deserves approbation*
228 Produce: *carry forth*
230 order: *course*

[*Aside to Brutus.*] You know not what you do; do not
    consent   232
That Antony speak in his funeral:
Know you how much the people may be mov'd
By that which he will utter?

    Bru.   By your pardon;
I will myself into the pulpit first,   236
And show the reason of our Cæsar's death:
What Antony shall speak, I will protest
He speaks by leave and by permission,
And that we are contented Cæsar shall   240
Have all true rites and lawful ceremonies.
It shall advantage more than do us wrong.

    Cas. I know not what may fall; I like it not.

    Bru. Mark Antony, here, take you Cæsar's
    body.   244
You shall not in your funeral speech blame us,
But speak all good you can devise of Cæsar,
And say you do 't by our permission;
Else shall you not have any hand at all   248
About his funeral; and you shall speak
In the same pulpit whereto I am going,
After my speech is ended.

    Ant.   Be it so;
I do desire no more.   252

    Bru. Prepare the body then, and follow us.
                 Exeunt all but Antony.

    Ant. O pardon me, thou bleeding piece of earth,
That I am meek and gentle with these butchers;
Thou art the ruins of the noblest man   256
That ever lived in the tide of times.
Woe to the hand that shed this costly blood!

235 By . . . pardon: *pardon me a moment, and I'll explain*
238 protest: *announce*
257 tide of times: *ebb and flow of human existence*

Over thy wounds now do I prophesy,—
Which like dumb mouths do ope their ruby lips,   260
To beg the voice and utterance of my tongue,—
A curse shall light upon the limbs of men;
Domestic fury and fierce civil strife
Shall cumber all the parts of Italy;   264
Blood and destruction shall be so in use,
And dreadful objects so familiar,
That mothers shall but smile when they behold
Their infants quarter'd with the hands of war,—
All pity chok'd with custom of fell deeds;   269
And Cæsar's spirit, ranging for revenge,
With Ate by his side come hot from hell,
Shall in these confines with a monarch's voice
Cry 'Havoc!' and let slip the dogs of war;   273
That this foul deed shall smell above the earth
With carrion men, groaning for burial.

Enter Octavius' Servant.

You serve Octavius Cæsar, do you not?   276
   Serv. I do, Mark Antony.
   Ant. Cæsar did write for him to come to Rome.
   Serv. He did receive his letters, and is coming;
And bid me say to you by word of mouth—   280
                              [*Seeing the body.*]
O Cæsar!—
   Ant. Thy heart is big, get thee apart and weep.
Passion, I see, is catching; for mine eyes,
Seeing those beads of sorrow stand in thine,   284
Began to water.   Is thy master coming?

268 quarter'd: *hewn into pieces*
269 custom . . . deeds: *the mere frequency of cruel actions*
271 Ate: *goddess of discord*   272 confines: *regions*
273 Havoc: *the signal for killing without sparing*
        dogs of war; *cf. n.*   let slip: *unleash*
                                                274 That: *so that*
275 *With rotting corpses, too numerous for the burial that they*
        grievously demand   283 Passion: *emotion*

Serv. He lies to-night within seven leagues of Rome.

Ant. Post back with speed, and tell him what hath chanc'd:

Here is a mourning Rome, a dangerous Rome,   288
No Rome of safety for Octavius yet;
Hie hence and tell him so. Yet, stay awhile;
Thou shalt not back till I have borne this corpse
Into the market-place; there shall I try,   292
In my oration, how the people take
The cruel issue of these bloody men;
According to the which thou shalt discourse
To young Octavius of the state of things.   296
Lend me your hand.   *Exeunt [with Cæsar's body].*

Scene Two

[*The Forum*]

Enter Brutus and [presently] goes into the Pulpit, and Cassius, with the Plebeians.

Plebeians. We will be satisfied: let us be satisfied.
Bru. Then follow me, and give me audience, friends.
Cassius, go you into the other street,
And part the numbers.   4
Those that will hear me speak, let 'em stay here;
Those that will follow Cassius, go with him;
And public reasons shall be rendered
Of Cæsar's death.
   First Ple.   I will hear Brutus speak.   8
   Sec. Ple. I will hear Cassius, and compare their reasons,

294 issue: *deed*   295 the which: *the way in which people act*
4 *And divide the throng*

When severally we hear them rendered.

      [Exit Cassius, with some of the Plebeians.]
Third Ple. The noble Brutus is ascended: silence!
Bru. Be patient till the last.   12
Romans, countrymen, and lovers, hear me for
my cause, and be silent, that you may hear:
believe me for mine honour, and have respect to
mine honour, that you may believe: censure me
in your wisdom, and awake your senses, that
you may the better judge. If there be any in this
assembly, any dear friend of Cæsar's, to him I
say, that Brutus' love to Cæsar was no less than 20
his. If then that friend demand why Brutus
rose against Cæsar, this is my answer: Not that
I loved Cæsar less, but that I loved Rome more.
Had you rather Cæsar were living, and die all
slaves, than that Cæsar were dead, to live all free
men? As Cæsar loved me, I weep for him; as
he was fortunate, I rejoice at it; as he was
valiant, I honour him; but, as he was ambitious, 28
I slew him. There is tears, for his love; joy, for
his fortune; honour, for his valour; and death,
for his ambition. Who is here so base that
would be a bondman? If any, speak; for him
have I offended. Who is here so rude that 33
would not be a Roman? If any, speak; for him
have I offended. Who is here so vile that will
not love his country? If any, speak; for him
have I offended. I pause for a reply.   37
    All. None, Brutus, none.
    Bru. Then none have I offended. I have
done no more to Cæsar, than you shall do to
Brutus. The question of his death is enrolled

12 *Give me a patient hearing, till I finish*   33 rude: *uncivilized*
41 question of: *official inquest into*   enrolled: *recorded*

in the Capitol; his glory not extenuated, wherein he was worthy, nor his offences enforced, for
which he suffered death.   44

        Enter Mark Antony, with Cæsar's body.

Here comes his body, mourned by Mark Antony:
who, though he had no hand in his death, shall
receive the benefit of his dying, a place in the
commonwealth; as which of you shall not?
With this I depart: that, as I slew my best lover
for the good of Rome, I have the same dagger
for myself, when it shall please my country to
need my death.   52

    All. Live, Brutus! live! live!

    First Ple. Bring him with triumph home unto his
      house.

    Sec. Ple. Give him a statue with his ancestors.

    Third Ple. Let him be Cæsar.

    Fourth Ple.   Cæsar's better parts
Shall be crown'd in Brutus.   57

    First Ple. We'll bring him to his house with shouts
      and clamours.

    Bru. My countrymen,—

    Sec. Ple.   Peace! silence! Brutus speaks.

    First Ple. Peace, ho!   60

    Bru. Good countrymen, let me depart alone,
And, for my sake, stay here with Antony.
Do grace to Cæsar's corpse, and grace his speech
Tending to Cæsar's glories, which Mark Antony,
By our permission, is allow'd to make.   65
I do entreat you, not a man depart,
Save I alone, till Antony have spoke.   *Exit.*

    First Ple. Stay, ho! and let us hear Mark An-
    tony.   68

---

42 extenuated: *belittled*   **43** enforced: *unduly stressed, strained*

Third Ple. Let him go up into the public chair;
We'll hear him.   Noble Antony, go up.
Ant. For Brutus' sake, I am beholding to you.
                                        [*Goes up.*]
Fourth Ple. What does he say of Brutus?
Third Ple.   He says, for Brutus' sake,
He finds himself beholding to us all.   73
Fourth Ple. 'Twere best he speak no harm of
   Brutus here.
First Ple. This Cæsar was a tyrant.
Third Ple.   Nay, that's certain:
We are bless'd that Rome is rid of him.   76
Sec. Ple. Peace! let us hear what Antony can say.
Ant. You gentle Romans,—
All.   Peace, ho! let us hear him.
Ant. Friends, Romans, countrymen, lend me your
   ears;
I come to bury Cæsar, not to praise him.   80
The evil that men do lives after them,
The good is oft interred with their bones;
So let it be with Cæsar.   The noble Brutus
Hath told you Cæsar was ambitious;   84
If it were so, it was a grievous fault,
And grievously hath Cæsar answer'd it.
Here, under leave of Brutus and the rest,—
For Brutus is an honourable man;   88
So are they all, all honourable men,—
Come I to speak in Cæsar's funeral.
He was my friend, faithful and just to me:
But Brutus says he was ambitious;   92
And Brutus is an honourable man.
He hath brought many captives home to Rome,
Whose ransoms did the general coffers fill:

71 beholding: *indebted*   86 answer'd: *atoned for*
95 general coffers: *public treasury*

Did this in Cæsar seem ambitious?   96
When that the poor have cried, Cæsar hath wept;
Ambition should be made of sterner stuff:
Yet Brutus says he was ambitious;
And Brutus is an honourable man.   100
You all did see that on the Lupercal
I thrice presented him a kingly crown,
Which he did thrice refuse: was this ambition?
Yet Brutus says he was ambitious;   104
And, sure, he is an honourable man.
I speak not to disprove what Brutus spoke,
But here I am to speak what I do know.
You all did love him once, not without cause: 108
What cause withholds you then to mourn for him?
O judgment, thou art fled to brutish beasts,
And men have lost their reason.   Bear with me;
My heart is in the coffin there with Cæsar,   112
And I must pause till it come back to me.
　　First Ple. Methinks there is much reason in his
　　　sayings.
　　Sec. Ple. If thou consider rightly of the matter,
Cæsar has had great wrong.
　　Third Ple.   Has he, masters?   116
I fear there will a worse come in his place.
　　Fourth Ple. Mark'd ye his words?   He would not
　　　take the crown;
Therefore 'tis certain he was not ambitious.
　　First Ple. If it be found so, some will dear abide
　　　it.   120
　　Sec. Ple. Poor soul, his eyes are red as fire with
　　　weeping.
　　Third Ple. There's not a nobler man in Rome than
　　　Antony.

101 on the Lupercal: *on the day of the Lupercalia*

Fourth Ple. Now mark him; he begins again to
    speak.

Ant. But yesterday the word of Cæsar might   124
Have stood against the world; now lies he there,
And none so poor to do him reverence.
O masters, if I were dispos'd to stir
Your hearts and minds to mutiny and rage,   128
I should do Brutus wrong, and Cassius wrong,
Who, you all know, are honourable men.
I will not do them wrong; I rather choose
To wrong the dead, to wrong myself, and you,   132
Than I will wrong such honourable men.
But here's a parchment with the seal of Cæsar;
I found it in his closet; 'tis his will.
Let but the commons hear this testament—   136
Which, pardon me, I do not mean to read—
And they would go and kiss dead Cæsar's wounds,
And dip their napkins in his sacred blood,
Yea, beg a hair of him for memory,   140
And, dying, mention it within their wills,
Bequeathing it as a rich legacy
Unto their issue.

Fourth Ple. We'll hear the will: read it, Mark
    Antony.   144

All. The will, the will! we will hear Cæsar's will!

Ant. Have patience, gentle friends; I must not
    read it:
It is not meet you know how Cæsar lov'd you.
You are not wood, you are not stones, but men:
And, being men, hearing the will of Cæsar,   149
It will inflame you, it will make you mad.

124, 125 word . . . world: *his bare assertion would have carried his
    point against the world*
126 *And there are none so humble as to show him any respect*
136 commons: *common people*
139 napkins: *handkerchiefs*

'Tis good you know not that you are his heirs;
For if you should, O what would come of it?

   Fourth Ple. Read the will! we'll hear it, An-
     tony;   153
You shall read us the will, Cæsar's will.

   Ant. Will you be patient? Will you stay awhile?
I have o'ershot myself to tell you of it.   156
I fear I wrong the honourable men
Whose daggers have stabb'd Cæsar; I do fear it.

   Fourth Ple. They were traitors: honourable men!

   All. The will! the testament!   160

   Sec. Ple. They were villains, murderers. The will!
     read the will.

   Ant. You will compel me then to read the will?
Then make a ring about the corpse of Cæsar,
And let me show you him that made the will.   16*4*
Shall I descend? And will you give me leave?

   All. Come down.

   Sec. Ple. Descend.

   Third Ple. You shall have leave.   168

   Fourth Ple. A ring; stand round.

   First Ple. Stand from the hearse; stand from the
     body.   [*Antony comes down.*]

   Sec. Ple. Room for Antony, most noble Antony.

   Ant. Nay, press not so upon me; stand far off.   172

   All. Stand back! room! bear back!

   Ant. If you have tears, prepare to shed them now.
You all do know this mantle: I remember
The first time ever Cæsar put it on;   176
'Twas on a summer's evening, in his tent,
That day he overcame the Nervii.
Look, in this place ran Cassius' dagger through:
See what a rent the envious Casca made: 180

178 That day: *on the day on which; cf. n.*

Through this the well-beloved Brutus stabb'd;
And, as he pluck'd his cursed steel away,
Mark how the blood of Cæsar follow'd it,
As rushing out of doors, to be resolv'd   184
If Brutus so unkindly knock'd or no;
For Brutus, as you know, was Cæsar's angel:
Judge, O you gods, how dearly Cæsar lov'd him.
This was the most unkindest cut of all;   188
For when the noble Cæsar saw him stab,
Ingra..tude, more strong than traitors' arms,
Quite vanquish'd him: then burst his mighty heart;
And, in his mantle muffling up his face,   192
Even at the base of Pompey's statue,
Which all the while ran blood, great Cæsar fell.
O, what a fall was there, my countrymen!
Then I, and you, and all of us fell down,   196
Whilst bloody treason flourish'd over us.
O now you weep, and I perceive you feel
The dint of pity; these are gracious drops.
Kind souls, what, weep you when you but behold   200
Our Cæsar's vesture wounded? Look you here,
Here is himself, marr'd, as you see, with traitors.

   First Ple. O piteous spectacle!
   Sec. Ple. O noble Cæsar!   204
   Third Ple. C woeful day!
   Fourth Ple. O traitors! villains!
   First Ple. O most bloody sight!
   Sec. Ple. We will be revenged.   208
   [*All.*] Revenge!—About!—Seek!—Burn!
Fire!—Kill!—Slay! Let not a traitor live!
   Ant. Stay, countrymen,—
   First Ple. Peace there! Hear the noble Antony.

186 angel: *dear as his guardian spirit*
199 dint: *impression*

Sec. Ple. We'll hear him, we'll follow him, we'll die with him! 213

Ant. Good friends, sweet friends, let me not stir you up
To such a sudden flood of mutiny.
They that have done this deed are honourable:
What private griefs they have, alas, I know not, 217
That made them do it; they are wise and honourable,
And will, no doubt, with reasons answer you.
I come not, friends, to steal away your hearts:
I am no orator, as Brutus is; 221
But, as you know me all, a plain blunt man,
That love my friend; and that they know full well
That gave me public leave to speak of him.
For I have neither wit, nor words, nor worth, 225
Action, nor utterance, nor the power of speech,
To stir men's blood: I only speak right on;
I tell you that which you yourselves do know,
Show you sweet Cæsar's wounds, poor poor dumb mouths, 229
And bid them speak for me: but were I Brutus,
And Brutus Antony, there were an Antony
Would ruffle up your spirits, and put a tongue
In every wound of Cæsar, that should move 233
The stones of Rome to rise and mutiny.

All. We'll mutiny.

First Ple. We'll burn the house of Brutus.

Third Ple. Away, then! Come, seek the conspirators. 237

Ant. Yet hear me, countrymen; yet hear me speak.

All. Peace, ho!—Hear Antony, most noble Antony!

226 Action, nor utterance: *orator's powers of gesticulation and elocution*
227 right on: *with simple straightforwardness*   232 ruffle: *stir*

Ant. Why, friends, you go to do you know not
    what. 240
Wherein hath Cæsar thus deserv'd your loves?
Alas, you know not: I must tell you then.
You have forgot the will I told you of.

All. Most true. The will! Let's stay and hear
    the will. 244

Ant. Here is the will, and under Cæsar's seal.
To every Roman citizen he gives,
To every several man, seventy-five drachmas.

Sec. Ple. Most noble Cæsar! We'll revenge his
    death. 248

Third Ple. O royal Cæsar!

Ant. Hear me with patience.

All. Peace, ho!

Ant. Moreover, he hath left you all his walks, 252
His private arbours, and new-planted orchards,
On this side Tiber; he hath left them you,
And to your heirs for ever; common pleasures,
To walk abroad and recreate yourselves. 256
Here was a Cæsar! When comes such another?

First Ple. Never, never! Come, away, away!
We'll burn his body in the holy place,
And with the brands fire the traitors' houses.
Take up the body. 261

Sec. Ple. Go fetch fire.

Third Ple. Pluck down benches.

Fourth Ple. Pluck down forms, windows, any-
    thing.   *Exeunt Plebeians* [*with the body*].

Ant. Now let it work: mischief, thou art afoot; 265
Take thou what course thou wilt!

Enter Servant.

247 drachmas: *Greek coins; cf. n.*   254 this; *cf. n.*
255 pleasures: *pleasure-grounds* (*in which*)   264 forms: *long seats*

How now, fellow!

Serv. Sir, Octavius is already come to Rome.

Ant. Where is he?   268

Serv. He and Lepidus are at Cæsar's house.

Ant. And thither will I straight to visit him.
He comes upon a wish.   Fortune is merry,
And in this mood will give us anything.   272

Serv. I heard him say Brutus and Cassius
Are rid like madmen through the gates of Rome.

Ant. Belike they had some notice of the people, 275
How I had mov'd them.   Bring me to Octavius.

Exeunt.

Scene Three

[*A Street*]

Enter Cinna, the Poet, and after him the Plebeians.

Cin. I dreamt to-night that I did feast with Cæsar,
And things unluckily charge my fantasy:
I have no will to wander forth of doors,
Yet something leads me forth.   4

First Ple. What is your name?

Sec. Ple. Whither are you going?

Third Ple. Where do you dwell?

Fourth Ple. Are you a married man, or a
bachelor?   9

Sec. Ple. Answer every man directly.

First Ple. Ay, and briefly.

Fourth Ple. Ay, and wisely.   12

Third Ple. Ay, and truly, you were best.

Cin. What is my name?   Whither am I

271 upon a wish: *as if at my wish*
2 unluckily . . . fantasy: *weigh upon my fancy ominously*
13 you were best: *it would be best for you*

going? Where do I dwell? Am I a married
man, or a bachelor? Then, to answer every
man directly and briefly, wisely and truly:
wisely I say, I am a bachelor.   18

Sec. Ple. That's as much as to say, they are
fools that marry; you'll bear me a bang for
that, I fear. Proceed; directly.   21

Cin. Directly, I am going to Cæsar's funeral.

First Ple. As a friend or an enemy?

Cin. As a friend.   24

Sec. Ple. That matter is answered directly.

Fourth Ple. For your dwelling, briefly?

Cin. Briefly, I dwell by the Capitol.

Third Ple. Your name, sir, truly?   28

Cin. Truly, my name is Cinna.

Sec. Ple. Tear him to pieces; he's a conspirator!

Cin. I am Cinna the poet, I am Cinna the
poet!   33

Fourth Ple. Tear him for his bad verses, tear
him for his bad verses!

Cin. I am not Cinna the conspirator!

Sec. Ple. It is no matter, his name's Cinna;
pluck but his name out of his heart, ana turn
him going.   39

Third Ple. Tear him, tear him! Come,
brands, ho! Firebrands! To Brutus', to Cassius';
burn all. Some to Decius' house, and some to
Casca's; some to Ligarius'. Away! Go!   43

Exeunt all the Plebeians.

20 bear me a bang: *get a blow from me*
26 For: *now for*

ACT FOURTH

Scene One

[A Room in Antony's House]

Antony, Octavius, and Lepidus [seated at a table].

Ant. These many then shall die; their names are prick'd.

Oct. Your brother too must die; consent you, Lepidus?

Lep. I do consent.

Oct.   Prick him down, Antony.

Lep. Upon condition Publius shall not live,   4
Who is your sister's son, Mark Antony.

Ant. He shall not live; look, with a spot I damn him.

But, Lepidus, go you to Cæsar's house;
Fetch the will hither, and we shall determine   8
How to cut off some charge in legacies.

Lep. What, shall I find you here?

Oct. Or here or at the Capitol.   *Exit Lepidus.*

Ant. This is a slight unmeritable man,   12
Meet to be sent on errands: is it fit,
The three-fold world divided, he should stand
One of the three to share it?

Oct.   So you thought him;
And took his voice who should be prick'd to die,   16
In our black sentence and proscription.

Ant. Octavius, I have seen more days than you:

6 with . . . him: *by a mark 'pricked' opposite his name, I condemn him*
9 cut . . . charge: *reduce some expenditures (by killing the legatees)*
12 unmeritable: *without merit*
14 The . . . divided: *if the world is to be divided into three parts*
17 *In the black sentence of our proscription*

And though we lay these honours on this man,
To ease ourselves of divers slanderous loads, 20
He shall but bear them as the ass bears gold,
To groan and sweat under the business,
Either led or driven, as we point the way;
And having brought our treasure where we will, 24
Then take we down his load, and turn him off,
Like to the empty ass, to shake his ears,
And graze in commons.

    Oct.   You may do your will;
But he's a tried and valiant soldier. 28

    Ant. So is my horse, Octavius; and for that
I do appoint him store of provender.
It is a creature that I teach to fight,
To wind, to stop, to run directly on, 32
His corporal motion govern'd by my spirit.
And, in some taste, is Lepidus but so;
He must be taught, and train'd, and bid go forth;
A barren-spirited fellow; one that feeds 36
On objects, arts, and imitations
Which, out of use and stal'd by other men,
Begin his fashion: do not talk of him
But as a property. And now, Octavius, 40
Listen great things: Brutus and Cassius
Are levying powers; we must straight make head;
Therefore let our alliance be combin'd,
Our best friends made, and our best means stretch'd
    out; 44

26 empty: *unladen, worthless*   27 commons: *public pasture*
30 appoint: *assign*   32 wind: *turn*
34 taste: *measure, degree*   36 barren-spirited: *lacking initiative*
37 objects: *objects of interest, in general; cf. n.*   arts: *works of art;
    cf. n.*   imitations: *conventional forms, empty counterfeits*
38 stal'd: *outworn, made stale*
39 Begin his fashion: *are to him the height of fashion*
40 property: *instrument, tool*   41 Listen: *hear*
42 powers: *armed forces*   make head: *raise an army*
43 combin'd: *confirmed*
44 made: *made sure*   stretch'd out: *strained to the utmost*

And let us presently go sit in council,
How covert matters may be best disclos'd,
And open perils surest answered.

 Oct. Let us do so: for we are at the stake, 48
And bay'd about with many enemies;
And some that smile have in their hearts, I fear,
Millions of mischiefs.   *Exeunt.*

Scene Two

[*Camp near Sardis. Before Brutus' Tent*]

Drum. Enter Brutus, Lucilius, [Lucius,] and the
  Army. Titinius and Pindarus meet them.

 Bru. Stand, ho!
 Lucil. Give the word, ho! and stand!
 Bru. What now, Lucilius! is Cassius near?
 Lucil. He is at hand; and Pindarus is come 4
To do you salutation from his master.
 Bru. He greets me well. Your master, Pindarus,
In his own change, or by ill officers,
Hath given me some worthy cause to wish 8
Things done, undone; but, if he be at hand,
I shall be satisfied.
 Pin.   I do not doubt
But that my noble master will appear
Such as he is, full of regard and honour. 12
 Bru. He is not doubted. A word, Lucilius;
How he receiv'd you, let me be resolv'd.
 Lucil. With courtesy and with respect enough;

46 covert: *hidden* disclos'd: *discovered*
47 answered: *faced, met*   48, 49 *Cf. n.*
1 Stand: *halt* 2 Give the word: *pass along the command*
7 *Owing to a change in himself, or through misconduct of subordi-*
 nates 12 full . . . honour: *worthy of honorable regard*

But not with such familiar instances,   16
Nor with such free and friendly conference,
As he hath us'd of old.
    Bru.   Thou hast describ'd
A hot friend cooling. Ever note, Lucilius,
When love begins to sicken and decay,   20
It useth an enforced ceremony.
There are no tricks in plain and simple faith;
But hollow men, like horses hot at hand,
Make gallant show and promise of their mettle;   24
But when they should endure the bloody spur,
They fall their crests, and, like deceitful jades,
Sink in the trial. Comes his army on?
    Lucil. They mean this night in Sardis to be
        quarter'd;   28
The greater part, the horse in general,
Are come with Cassius.
    Bru.   Hark! he is arriv'd.
                      Low march within.
March gently on to meet him.

        Enter Cassius and his Powers.

    Cas. Stand, ho!   32
    Bru. Stand, ho! Speak the word along.
    [*First Officer.*] Stand!
    [*Sec. Officer.*] Stand!
    [*Third Officer.*] Stand!   36
    Cas. Most noble brother, you have done me wrong.
    Bru. Judge me, you gods! Wrong I mine enemies?
And, if not so, how should I wrong a brother?

16 familiar instances: *marks of familiarity*
23 hollow: *insincere*   hot at hand: *fiery at the start, only*
26 fall: *let fall, lower*   jades: *worthless nags*
27 Sink . . . trial: *fail in the pinch*
29 the horse in general: *all the cavalry*
31 gently: *slowly*

Cas. Brutus, this sober form of yours hides
    wrongs;   40
And when you do them—
Bru.   Cassius, be content;
Speak your griefs softly: I do know you well.
Before the eyes of both our armies here,
Which should perceive nothing but love from us,   44
Let us not wrangle: bid them move away;
Then in my tent, Cassius, enlarge your griefs,
And I will give you audience.
Cas.   Pindarus,
Bid our commanders lead their charges off   48
A little from this ground.
Bru. Lucilius, do you the like; and let no man
Come to our tent till we have done our conference.
Let Lucius and Titinius guard our door.   52
                                  Exeunt.

Scene Three

[Within the Tent of Brutus]

[Enter] Brutus and Cassius.

Cas. That you have wrong'd me doth appear in
    this:
You have condemn'd and noted Lucius Pella
For taking bribes here of the Sardians;
Wherein my letters, praying on his side,   4
Because I knew the man, were slighted off.
Bru. You wrong'd yourself to write in such a case.
Cas. In such a time as this it is not meet

---

40 sober form: *calm behavior*   42 softly: *gently*
46 enlarge: *set forth fully*   Scene Three S. d.; *cf. n.*
2 noted: *stigmatized*   4 praying . . . side:*interceding for him*
5 slighted off: *tossed slightingly aside*

That every nice offence should bear his comment.　8

　　Bru. Let me tell you, Cassius, you yourself
Are much condemn'd to have an itching palm;
To sell and mart your offices for gold
To undeservers.

　　Cas.　　　　　　I an itching palm!　12
You know that you are Brutus that speaks this,
Or, by the gods, this speech were else your last.

　　Bru. The name of Cassius honours this corruption,
And chastisement doth therefore hide his head.

　　Cas. Chastisement!　17

　　Bru. Remember March, the ides of March remember:
Did not great Julius bleed for justice' sake?
What villain touch'd his body, that did stab,　20
And not for justice?　What! shall one of us,
That struck the foremost man of all this world
But for supporting robbers, shall we now
Contaminate our fingers with base bribes,　24
And sell the mighty space of our large honours
For so much trash as may be grasped thus?
I had rather be a dog, and bay the moon,
Than such a Roman.

　　Cas.　　　　　　Brutus, bay not me;　28
I'll not endure it: you forget yourself,
To hedge me in.　I am a soldier, I,
Older in practice, abler than yourself
To make conditions.

　　Bru.　　　　　Go to; you are not, Cassius.　32

8 nice: *trivial*　　bear . . . comment: *be censured*
10 condemn'd to have: *blamed for having*　　11 mart: *market*
15 honours . . . corruption: *sanctions this corrupt practice*
20, 21 What . . . justice; *cf. n.*
23 robbers: *his dishonest favorites*
25, 26 *Cf. n.*　　　　　　　　　　　　27 bay: *bark at*
28 *Cf. n.*　　　　　　　　　31 practice: *experience*
32 make conditions: *determine the proper treatment of subordinates*
　　(*referring to lines 1-5*)　　Go to: *Nonsense!*

Cas. I am.

Bru. I say you are not.

Cas. Urge me no more, I shall forget myself;
Have mind upon your health; tempt me no further.   36

Bru. Away, slight man!

Cas. Is 't possible?

Bru.   Hear me, for I will speak.
Must I give way and room to your rash choler?
Shall I be frighted when a madman stares?   40

Cas. O ye gods, ye gods! Must I endure all this?

Bru. All this! ay, more: fret till your proud heart break;
Go show your slaves how choleric you are,
And make your bondmen tremble. Must I budge?   44
Must I observe you? Must I stand and crouch
Under your testy humour? By the gods,
You shall digest the venom of your spleen,
Though it do split you; for, from this day forth,   48
I'll use you for my mirth, yea, for my laughter,
When you are waspish.

Cas.   Is it come to this?

Bru. You say you are a better soldier:
Let it appear so; make your vaunting true,   52
And it shall please me well. For mine own part,
I shall be glad to learn of noble men.

Cas. You wrong me every way; you wrong me, Brutus;
I said an elder soldier, not a better: 56
Did I say, 'better'?

Bru.   If you did, I care not.

Cas. When Cæsar liv'd, he durst not thus have mov'd me.

36 Have . . . health: *have regard for your safety*
44 budge: *flinch*   45 observe: *pay humble reverence to*

Bru. Peace, peace! you durst not so have tempted
    him.

Cas. I durst not?   60

Bru. No.

Cas. What, durst not tempt him?

Bru.   For your life you durst not.

Cas. Do not presume too much upon my love;
I may do that I shall be sorry for.   64

Bru. You have done that you should be sorry for.
There is no terror, Cassius, in your threats;
For I am arm'd so strong in honesty
That they pass by me as the idle wind,   68
Which I respect not. I did send to you
For certain sums of gold, which you denied me;
For I can raise no money by vile means:
By heaven, I had rather coin my heart,   72
And drop my blood for drachmas, than to wring
From the hard hands of peasants their vile trash
By any indirection. I did send
To you for gold to pay my legions,   76
Which you denied me: was that done like Cassius?
Should I have answer'd Caius Cassius so?
When Marcus Brutus grows so covetous,
To lock such rascal counters from his friends, 80
Be ready, gods, with all your thunderbolts;
Dash him to pieces!

Cas.   I denied you not.

Bru. You did.

Cas.   I did not: he was but a fool
That brought my answer back. Brutus hath riv'd
    my heart.   84
A friend should bear his friend's infirmities,

69 respect: *heed*
75 indirection: *dishonesty, crooked dealing*
80 rascal counters: *worthless pelf*   84 riv'd: *cleft*

But Brutus makes mine greater than they are.

    Bru. I do not, till you practise them on me.

    Cas. You love me not.

    Bru.   I do not like your faults.   88

    Cas. A friendly eye could never see such faults.

    Bru. A flatterer's would not, though they do appear
As huge as high Olympus.

    Cas. Come, Antony, and young Octavius, come, 92
Revenge yourselves alone on Cassius,
For Cassius is aweary of the world;
Hated by one he loves; brav'd by his brother;
Check'd like a bondman; all his faults observ'd, 96
Set in a note-book, learn'd, and conn'd by rote,
To cast into my teeth. O, I could weep
My spirit from mine eyes. There is my dagger,
And here my naked breast; within, a heart   100
Dearer than Pluto's mine, richer than gold:
If that thou be'st a Roman, take it forth;
I, that denied thee gold, will give my heart:
Strike, as thou didst at Cæsar; for, I know, 104
When thou didst hate him worst, thou lov'dst him
    better
Than ever thou lov'dst Cassius.

    Bru.   Sheathe your dagger:
Be angry when you will, it shall have scope;
Do what you will, dishonour shall be humour. 108
O Cassius, you are yoked with a lamb
That carries anger as the flint bears fire,
Who, much enforced, shows a hasty spark,
And straight is cold again.

95 brav'd: *blusteringly taunted*   96 Check'd: *scolded*
97 learn'd . . . rote: *studied, and learned by heart*
101 Dearer: *worth more*   Pluto's; *cf. n.*
107 it . . . scope: *your anger shall not be opposed*
108 dishonour . . . humour: *your dishonorable deeds shall be ig-
nored as caprices*   109-112 *Cf. n.*

 Cas.   Hath Cassius liv'd   112
To be but mirth and laughter to his Brutus,
When grief and blood ill-temper'd vexeth him?
 Bru. When I spoke that I was ill-temper'd too.
 Cas. Do you confess so much? Give me your
  hand.   116
 Bru. And my heart too.
 Cas.   O Brutus!
 Bru.   What's the matter?
 Cas. Have not you love enough to bear with me,
When that rash humour which my mother gave me
Makes me forgetful?
 Bru.   Yes, Cassius; and from henceforth
When you are over-earnest with your Brutus,   121
He'll think your mother chides, and leave you so.
 Poet. [*Within.*] Let me go in to see the generals;
There is some grudge between 'em, 'tis not meet
They be alone.   125
 Lucil. [*Within.*] You shall not come to them.
 Poet. [*Within.*] Nothing but death shall stay me.

*Enter a Poet [followed by Lucilius, Titinius, and
Lucius].*

 Cas. How now! What's the matter?   128
 Poet. For shame, you generals! What do you
  mean?
Love, and be friends, as two such men should be;
For I have seen more years, I'm sure, than ye.
 Cas. Ha, ha! how vilely doth this cynic rime!
 Bru. Get you hence, sirrah; saucy fellow,
  hence!   **133**
 Cas. Bear with him, Brutus; 'tis his fashion.

114 blood ill-temper'd: *disordered condition*
132 cynic: *so called because Diogenes affected rudeness*

Bru. I'll know his humour, when he knows his
  time:
What should the wars do with these jigging
  fools?   136
Companion, hence!

  Cas.   Away, away: be gone!

                                              Exit Poet.

Bru. Lucilius and Titinius, bid the commanders
Prepare to lodge their companies to-night.

  Cas. And come yourselves, and bring Messala with
  you,   140
Immediately to us.

                    [*Exeunt Lucilius and Titinius.*]

  Bru.   Lucius, a bowl of wine! [*Exit Lucius.*]

  Cas. I did not think you could have been so angry.

  Bru. O Cassius, I am sick of many griefs.

  Cas. Of your philosophy you make no use,   144
If you give place to accidental evils.

  Bru. No man bears sorrow better: Portia is dead.

  Cas. Ha? Portia?

  Bru. She is dead.   148

  Cas. How 'scap'd I killing when I cross'd you so?
O insupportable and touching loss!
Upon what sickness?

  Bru.   Impatient of my absence,
And grief that young Octavius with Mark An-
  tony   152
Have made themselves so strong;—for with her death
That tidings came:—with this she fell distract,
And, her attendants absent, swallow'd fire.

135 *I'll listen to his folly when he learns the proper time for it*
136 jigging: *doggerel rhyming*
137 Companion: *base fellow*
139 lodge . . . to-night: *encamp for the night*
145 give . . . accidental: *admit the power of casual*
151 Upon: *of*   Impatient of: *unable to endure*
152 grief; *cf. n.*   154 fell distract: *became distracted*

Cas. And died so?

Bru.   Even so.

Cas.   O ye immortal gods!   156

   Enter Boy [Lucius], with wine and tapers.

Bru. Speak no more of her. Give me a bowl of
   wine.

In this I bury all unkindness, Cassius.   *Drinks.*

Cas. My heart is thirsty for that noble pledge.

Fill, Lucius, till the wine o'erswell the cup;   160

I cannot drink too much of Brutus' love.   *[Drinks.]*

   Bru. Come in, Titinius.   *[Exit Lucius.]*

     Enter Titinius and Messala.

                  Welcome, good Messala.

Now sit we close about this taper here,

And call in question our necessities.   164

   Cas. Portia, art thou gone?

   Bru.   No more, I pray you.

Messala, I have here received letters,

That young Octavius and Mark Antony

Come down upon us with a mighty power,   168

Bending their expedition towards Philippi.

   Mes. Myself have letters of the self-same tenour.

   Bru. With what addition?

   Mes. That by proscription and bills of out-
   lawry,   172

Octavius, Antony, and Lepidus,

Have put to death an hundred senators.

   Bru. Therein our letters do not well agree;

Mine speak of seventy senators that died   176

By their proscriptions, Cicero being one.

   Cas. Cicero one?

---

164 call in question: *bring up for discussion*
169 Bending . . . expedition: *directing their march*

Mes.   Cicero is dead,
And by that order of proscription.
Had you your letters from your wife, my lord?
    Bru. No, Messala.   181
    Mes. Nor nothing in your letters writ of her?
    Bru. Nothing, Messala.
    Mes.   That, methinks, is strange.
    Bru. Why ask you? Hear you aught of her in
      yours?   184
    Mes. No, my lord.
    Bru. Now, as you are a Roman, tell me true.
    Mes. Then like a Roman bear the truth I tell:
For certain she is dead, and by strange manner.
    Bru. Why, farewell, Portia. We must die, Mes-
      sala: 189
With meditating that she must die once,
I have the patience to endure it now.
    Mes. Even so great men great losses should en-
      dure.   192
    Cas. I have as much of this in art as you,
But yet my nature could not bear it so.
    Bru. Well, to our work alive. What do you think
Of marching to Philippi presently?   196
    Cas. I do not think it good.
    Bru.   Your reason?
    Cas.   This is it:
'Tis better that the enemy seek us:
So shall he waste his means, weary his soldiers,
Doing himself offence; whilst we, lying still,   200
Are full of rest, defence, and nimbleness.
    Bru. Good reasons must, of force, give place to
      better.

183 Nothing, Messala; *cf. n.*
190 once: *some day*   193 art: *theory*
195 alive: *which concerns the living*
202 force: *necessity*

The people 'twixt Philippi and this ground
Do stand but in a forc'd affection;   204
For they have grudg'd us contribution:
The enemy, marching along by them,
By them shall make a fuller number up,
Come on refresh'd, new-added, and encourag'd;
From which advantage shall we cut him off,   209
If at Philippi we do face him there,
These people at our back.

    Cas.   Hear me, good brother.

    Bru. Under your pardon. You must note be-
       side,   212
That we have tried the utmost of our friends,
Our legions are brim-full, our cause is ripe:
The enemy increaseth every day;
We, at the height, are ready to decline.   216
There is a tide in the affairs of men,
Which, taken at the flood, leads on to fortune;
Omitted, all the voyage of their life
Is bound in shallows and in miseries.   220
On such a full sea are we now afloat;
And we must take the current when it serves,
Or lose our ventures.

    Cas.   Then, with your will, go on;
We'll along ourselves, and meet them at Philippi.   224

    Bru. The deep of night is crept upon our talk,
And nature must obey necessity,
Which we will niggard with a little rest.
There is no more to say?

204 *Are friendly to us only under compulsion*
208 new-added: *newly augmented*
213 *That we have drawn on our friends to the utmost*
219 Omitted: *if it is neglected*
220 bound in: *confined to*
223 ventures: *investments*   with your will: *according to your prefer-
ence*
227 *So to nature's need we will dole out a little rest*

Cas.   No more.   Good-night: 228
Early to-morrow will we rise, and hence.
    Bru. Lucius!

Enter Lucius.

                    My gown.   [*Exit Lucius.*]
                    Farewell, good Messala:
Good-night, Titinius.   Noble, noble Cassius,
Good-night, and good repose.
    Cas.   O my dear brother! 232
This was an ill beginning of the night:
Never come such division 'tween our souls!
Let it not, Brutus.
    Bru.   Everything is well.
    Cas. Good-night, my lord.
    Bru.   Good-night, good brother. 236
    Tit. }
    Mes. } Good-night, Lord Brutus.
    Bru.   Farewell, every one.
                    Exeunt [*all but Brutus*].

Enter Lucius, with the gown.

Give me the gown.   Where is thy instrument?
    Luc. Here in the tent.
    Bru.   What, thou speak'st drowsily?
Poor knave, I blame thee not; thou art o'er-
        watch'd.   240
Call Claudius and some other of my men;
I'll have them sleep on cushions in my tent.
    Luc. Varro! and Claudius!

Enter Varro and Claudius.

    Var. Calls my lord?   244
    Bru. I pray you, sirs, lie in my tent and sleep:

240 knave: *boy*   o'er-watch'd: *worn out by lack of sleep*

It may be I shall raise you by and by
On business to my brother Cassius.

Var. So please you, we will stand and watch your
    pleasure.   248

Bru. I will not have it so; lie down, good sirs;
It may be I shall otherwise bethink me.

                    [Varro and Claudius lie down.]

Look, Lucius, here's the book I sought for so;
I put it in the pocket of my gown.   252

Luc. I was sure your lordship did not give it me.

Bru. Bear with me, good boy, I am much forgetful.
Canst thou hold up thy heavy eyes awhile,
And touch thy instrument a strain or two?   256

Luc. Ay, my lord, an 't please you.

Bru.   It does, my boy:
I trouble thee too much, but thou art willing.

Luc. It is my duty, sir.

Bru. I should not urge thy duty past thy
    might;   260
I know young bloods look for a time of rest.

Luc. I have slept, my lord, already.

Bru. It was well done, and thou shalt sleep again;
I will not hold thee long: if I do live,   264
I will be good to thee.   *Music, and a Song.*
This is a sleepy tune: O murderous slumber,
Lay'st thou thy leaden mace upon my boy,
That plays thee music? Gentle knave, good-
    night;   268
I will not do thee so much wrong to wake thee.
If thou dost nod, thou break'st thy instrument;
I'll take it from thee; and, good boy, good-night.

---

246 raise: *rouse*   248 watch: *wakefully await*
254 much: *very*
256 *Play a tune or two on thy lute*
266 murderous: *because rendering apparently lifeless*
267 leaden: *dull and heavy*   mace: *bailiff's staff for arresting people*

Let me see, let me see; is not the leaf turn'd
    down   272
Where I left reading?   Here it is, I think.

Enter the Ghost of Cæsar.

How ill this taper burns.   Ha!   Who comes here?
I think it is the weakness of mine eyes
That shapes this monstrous apparition.   276
It comes upon me.   Art thou anything?
Art thou some god, some angel, or some devil,
That mak'st my blood cold and my hair to stare?
Speak to me what thou art.   280
    Ghost. Thy evil spirit, Brutus.
    Bru.   Why com'st thou?
    Ghost. To tell thee thou shalt see me at Philippi.
    Bru. Well; then I shall see thee again?
    Ghost.   Ay, at Philippi.
    Bru. Why, I will see thee at Philippi then.   284
                            [Exit Ghost.]

Now I have taken heart, thou vanishest:
Ill spirit, I would hold more talk with thee.
Boy, Lucius!   Varro!   Claudius!   Sirs, awake!
Claudius!   288
    Luc. The strings, my lord, are false.
    Bru. He thinks he still is at his instrument.
Lucius, awake!
    Luc. My lord!   292
    Bru. Didst thou dream, Lucius, that thou so criedst
    out?
    Luc. My lord, I do not know that I did cry.
    Bru. Yes, that thou didst.   Didst thou see any-
    thing?
    Luc. Nothing, my lord.   296

274 How . . . burns: *accepted sign of an apparition's presence*
277 upon: *towards*   279 stare: *stand on end*

Bru. Sleep again, Lucius. Sirrah, Claudius!
Fellow thou, awake!
   Var. My lord!
   Clau. My lord!   300
   Bru. Why did you so cry out, sirs, in your sleep?
   Both. Did we, my lord?
   Bru.   Ay: saw you anything?
   Var. No, my lord, I saw nothing.
   Clau.   Nor I, my lord.
   Bru. Go, and commend me to my brother Cas-
      sius: 304
Bid him set on his powers betimes before,
And we will follow.
   Both. It shall be done, my lord.   *Exeunt.*

ACT FIFTH

Scene One

[*The Plains of Philippi*]

Enter Octavius, Antony, and their Army.

Oct. Now, Antony, our hopes are answered:
You said the enemy would not come down,
But keep the hills and upper regions;
It proves not so; their battles are at hand;   4
They mean to warn us at Philippi here,
Answering before we do demand of them.
   Ant. Tut, I am in their bosoms, and I know
Wherefore they do it: they could be content   8
To visit other places; and come down

1 answered: *fulfilled*   4 battles: *battalions*
5 warn: *summon, challenge*   7 bosoms: *secrets*

With fearful bravery, thinking by this face
To fasten in our thoughts that they have courage;
But 'tis not so.

Enter a Messenger.

Mess.   Prepare you, generals: **12**
The enemy comes on in gallant show;
Their bloody sign of battle is hung out,
And something to be done immediately.

Ant. Octavius, lead your battle softly on,   **16**
Upon the left hand of the even field.

Oct. Upon the right hand I; keep thou the left.

Ant. Why do you cross me in this exigent?

Oct. I do not cross you; but I will do so.   20
                                                  March.

Drum.   Enter Brutus, Cassius, and their Army.

Bru. They stand, and would have parley.

Cas. Stand fast, Titinius: we must out and talk.

Oct. Mark Antony, shall we give sign of battle?

Ant. No, Cæsar, we will answer on their
              charge.   24
Make forth; the generals would have some words.

Oct. [*To his troops.*] Stir not until the signal.

Bru. Words before blows: is it so, countrymen?

Oct. Not that we love words better, as you do.   28

Bru. Good words are better than bad strokes,
              Octavius.

Ant. In your bad strokes, Brutus, you give good
              words:

Witness the hole you made in Cæsar's heart,

10 fearful bravery: *cowardly bravado*   face: *pretense*
14 bloody . . . battle: *signal for immediate combat*
17 even: *equally divided*   19 exigent: *emergency*
20 but . . . so: *but I shall do as I said* 21 parley: *conference*
24 answer . . . charge: *fight when they attack*
25 Make forth: *step forward*
30 In . . . strokes: *while delivering foul blows*

Crying, 'Long live! Hail, Cæsar!'

   Cas.   Antony,   32

The posture of your blows are yet unknown;

But for your words, they rob the Hybla bees,

And leave them honeyless.

   Ant.   Not stingless too!

   Bru. O yes, and soundless too;   36

For you have stol'n their buzzing, Antony,

And very wisely threat before you sting.

   Ant. Villains! you did not so when your vile
      daggers

Hack'd one another in the sides of Cæsar: 40

You show'd your teeth like apes, and fawn'd like
      hounds,

And bow'd like bondmen, kissing Cæsar's feet;

Whilst damned Casca, like a cur, behind

Struck Cæsar on the neck. O you flatterers!   44

   Cas. Flatterers! Now, Brutus, thank yourself:

This tongue had not offended so to-day,

If Cassius might have rul'd.

   Oct. Come, come, the cause: if arguing make us
      sweat,   48

The proof of it will turn to redder drops.

Look:

I draw a sword against conspirators;

When think you that the sword goes up again?   52

Never, till Cæsar's three-and-thirty wounds

Be well aveng'd; or till another Cæsar

Have added slaughter to the sword of traitors.

   Bru. Cæsar, thou canst not die by traitors'
      hands,   56

33 posture: *nature (?)*   are: *a plural by attraction*
34 Hybla: *town in Sicily, famous for its honey*
41 show'd . . . apes: *simulated smiles of affection, like favorite pets*
44 flatterers: *treacherous hypocrites*
48 the cause: *let's get down to business*   53 three-and-thirty; *cf. n.*

Unless thou bring'st them with thee.

Oct.   So I hope;
I was not born to die on Brutus' sword.

Bru. O, if thou wert the noblest of thy strain,
Young man, thou couldst not die more honour-
able.   60

Cas. A peevish schoolboy, worthless of such honour,
Join'd with a masquer and a reveller.

Ant. Old Cassius still!

Oct.   Come, Antony; away!
Defiance, traitors, hurl we in your teeth.   64
If you dare fight to-day, come to the field;
If not, when you have stomachs.

                            Exeunt Octavius, Antony, and Army.

Cas. Why now, blow wind, swell billow, and swim
bark!
The storm is up, and all is on the hazard.   68

Bru. Ho, Lucilius: hark, a word with you.

Lucil. [*Standing forth.*]   My lord?
                            [*Brutus and Lucilius talk apart.*]

Cas. Messala.

Mes. [*Standing forth.*] What says my general?

Cas.   Messala,
This is my birth-day; as this very day   72
Was Cassius born. Give me thy hand, Messala:
Be thou my witness that against my will,
As Pompey was, am I compell'd to set
Upon one battle all our liberties.   76
You know that I held Epicurus strong,
And his opinion; now I change my mind,

59 strain: *race*
61 peevish: *silly*   such honour: *i.e., that of dying on Brutus' sword*
63 Old . . . still: *you are still the same old Cassius*
66 stomachs: *courage*
72 as: *a colloquial expletive*
75 As Pompey: *at the battle of Pharsalia, 48 B. C.*
77 held . . . strong: *believed Epicurus right in disregarding omens*

And partly credit things that do presage.
Coming from Sardis, on our former ensign   80
Two mighty eagles fell, and there they perch'd,
Gorging and feeding from our soldiers' hands;
Who to Philippi here consorted us:
This morning are they fled away and gone,   84
And in their stead do ravens, crows, and kites
Fly o'er our heads, and downward look on us,
As we were sickly prey: their shadows seem
A canopy most fatal, under which   88
Our army lies, ready to give up the ghost.
    Mes. Believe not so.
    Cas.   I but believe it partly,
For I am fresh of spirit and resolv'd
To meet all perils very constantly.   92
    Bru. Even so, Lucilius.
    Cas.   Now, most noble Brutus,
The gods to-day stand friendly, that we may,
Lovers in peace, lead on our days to age!
But since the affairs of men rest still incertain,   96
Let's reason with the worst that may befall.
If we do lose this battle, then is this
The very last time we shall speak together:
What are you, then, determined to do?   100
    Bru. Even by the rule of that philosophy
By which I did blame Cato for the death
Which he did give himself—(I know not how,
But I do find it cowardly and vile,   104
For fear of what might fall, so to prevent
The time of life)—arming myself with patience,

80 former ensign: *banner at the front of our column*
83 consorted: *accompanied*
87 As: *as if*   sickly prey: *so sick as soon to be their prey*
88 fatal: *fateful, doom-foreboding*
94 The gods: *may the gods*
97 reason with: *consider*
102 Cato: *of Utica; committed suicide, 46 B. C.*

To stay the providence of some high powers
That govern us below.

   Cas.   Then, if we lose this battle,   108
You are contented to be led in triumph
Thorough the streets of Rome?

   Bru. No, Cassius, no: think not, thou noble Roman,
That ever Brutus will go bound to Rome;   112
He bears too great a mind: but this same day
Must end that work the ides of March begun;
And whether we shall meet again I know not.
Therefore our everlasting farewell take: 116
For ever, and for ever, farewell, Cassius.
If we do meet again, why, we shall smile;
If not, why then this parting was well made.

   Cas. For ever, and for ever, farewell, Brutus.
If we do meet again, we'll smile indeed;   121
If not, 'tis true this parting was well made.

   Bru. Why, then, lead on. O, that a man might know
The end of this day's business, ere it come!   124
But it sufficeth that the day will end,
And then the end is known. Come, ho! away!

                                     Exeunt.

Scene Two

[*The Same. The Field of Battle*]

Alarum. Enter Brutus and Messala.

   Bru. Ride, ride, Messala, ride, and give these bills
Unto the legions on the other side.   *Loud alarum.*
Let them set on at once, for I perceive
But cold demeanour in Octavius' wing,   4

107 stay: *await, submit to*   111-115 *Cf. n.*
1 bills: *written orders*   2 side: *wing, commanded by Cassius*
4 cold demeanour: *faint-heartedness*

And sudden push gives them the overthrow.
Ride, ride, Messala: let them all come down.

Exeunt.

Scene Three

[*Another part of the Field*]

Alarums. Enter Cassius and Titinius.

Cas. O look, Titinius, look, the villains fly!
Myself have to mine own turn'd enemy:
This ensign here of mine was turning back;
I slew the coward, and did take it from him.   4

Tit. O Cassius! Brutus gave the word too early;
Who, having some advantage on Octavius,
Took it too eagerly: his soldiers fell to spoil,
Whilst we by Antony are all enclos'd.   8

Enter Pindarus.

Pin. Fly further off, my lord, fly further off;
Mark Antony is in your tents, my lord:
Fly, therefore, noble Cassius, fly far off.
Cas. This hill is far enough. Look, look, Ti-
    tinius;   12
Are those my tents where I perceive the fire?
Tit. They are, my lord.
Cas.   Titinius, if thou lovest me,
Mount thou my horse, and hide thy spurs in him,
Till he have brought thee up to yonder troops
And here again; that I may rest assur'd   17
Whether yond troops are friend or enemy.
Tit. I will be here again, even with a thought.

Exit.

2 mine own: *my own troops*
4 coward: *i.e., the standard-bearer*   19 even with: *quick as*

Cas. Go, Pindarus, get higher on that hill;
My sight was ever thick; regard Titinius,   21
And tell me what thou not'st about the field.

         [*Pindarus ascends the hill.*]

This day I breathed first; time is come round,
And where I did begin, there shall I end;   24
My life is run his compass. Sirrah, what news?

Pin. [*Above.*] O my lord!

Cas. What news?

Pin. [*Above.*] Titinius is enclosed round about   28
With horsemen, that make to him on the spur;
Yet he spurs on. Now they are almost on him:
Now, Titinius! Now some light; O, he lights too:
He's ta'en.   *Shout.*

     And hark, they shout for joy. 32

Cas. Come down; behold no more.
O, coward that I am, to live so long,
To see my best friend ta'en before my face!

     Enter Pindarus [*below*].

Come hither, sirrah: 36
In Parthia did I take thee prisoner;
And then I swore thee, saving of thy life,
That whatsoever I did bid thee do,
Thou shouldst attempt it. Come now, keep thine
  oath;   40
Now be a freeman; and with this good sword,
That ran through Cæsar's bowels, search this bosom.
Stand not to answer; here, take thou the hilts;
And, when my face is cover'd, as 'tis now,   44

21 thick: *dull, imperfect*
25 is . . . compass: *has completed its cycle*
31 light: *alight, dismount*
37 Parthia: *in Crassus' disastrous campaign, in 53 B. C.*
38 swore thee: *made thee swear* saving of: *in return for my sparing*
41 freeman: *Cassius' death will free him from slavery*
42 search: *probe*

Guide thou the sword.—Cæsar, thou art reveng'd,
Even with the sword that kill'd thee.   [*Dies.*]

Pin. So, I am free; yet would not so have been,
Durst I have done my will. O Cassius,   48
Far from this country Pindarus shall run,
Where never Roman shall take note of him.   *Exit.*

Enter Titinius and Messala.

Mes. It is but change, Titinius; for Octavius
Is overthrown by noble Brutus' power,   52
As Cassius' legions are by Antony.

Tit. These tidings will well comfort Cassius.

Mes. Where did you leave him?

Tit.   All disconsolate.
With Pindarus his bondman, on this hill.   56

Mes. Is not that he that lies upon the ground?

Tit. He lies not like the living. O my heart!

Mes. Is not that he?

Tit.   No, this was he, Messala.
But Cassius is no more. O setting sun,   60
As in thy red rays thou dost sink to night,
So in his red blood Cassius' day is set.
The sun of Rome is set. Our day is gone;
Clouds, dews, and dangers come; our deeds are
        done.   64
Mistrust of my success hath done this deed.

Mes. Mistrust of good success hath done this deed.
O hateful error, melancholy's child,
Why dost thou show to the apt thoughts of men   68
The things that are not? O error, soon conceiv'd,
Thou never com'st unto a happy birth,

50 take note of: *see*   51 change: *exchange*
64 our . . . done: *all is over*
65 Mistrust . . . success: *misgivings about the outcome of my errand*
67 melancholy's child: *result of despondency*
68 apt: *impressionable*

But kill'st the mother that engender'd thee.

   Tit. What, Pindarus! Where art thou, Pindarus?   72

   Mes. Seek him, Titinius, whilst I go to meet
The noble Brutus, thrusting this report
Into his ears; I may say, thrusting it:
For piercing steel and darts envenomed   76
Shall be as welcome to the ears of Brutus
As tidings of this sight.

   Tit.   Hie you, Messala,
And I will seek for Pindarus the while.

                                [Exit Messala.]

Why didst thou send me forth, brave Cassius?
Did I not meet thy friends, and did not they   81
Put on my brows this wreath of victory,
And bid me give it thee? Didst thou not hear their
    shouts?
Alas, thou hast misconstru'd everything.   84
But, hold thee, take this garland on thy brow;
Thy Brutus bid me give it thee, and I
Will do his bidding. Brutus, come apace,
And see how I regarded Caius Cassius.   88
By your leave, gods: this is a Roman's part:
Come, Cassius' sword, and find Titinius' heart.

                                     Dies.

Alarum. Enter Brutus, Messala, Young Cato, Strato,
Volumnius, and Lucilius.

   Bru. Where, where, Messala, doth his body lie?   91

   Mes. Lo, yonder: and Titinius mourning it.

   Bru. Titinius' face is upward.

   Cato.   He is slain.

   Bru. O Julius Cæsar, thou art mighty yet!

---

85 hold thee: *wait a moment*   87 apace: *quickly*
89 By . . . gods: a *proud apology for taking his fate into his own*
hands

Thy spirit walks abroad, and turns our swords
In our own proper entrails.   *Low alarums.*
   Cato.   Brave Titinius!   96
Look whether he have not crown'd dead Cassius!
   Bru. Are yet two Romans living such as these?
The last of all the Romans, fare thee well!
It is impossible that ever Rome   100
Should breed thy fellow.   Friends, I owe more tears
To this dead man than you shall see me pay.—
I shall find time, Cassius, I shall find time.—
Come therefore, and to Thasos send his body: 104
His funerals shall not be in our camp,
Lest it discomfort us.   Lucilius, come;
And come, young Cato;—let us to the field.
Labeo and Flavius, set our battles on: 108
'Tis three o'clock; and, Romans, yet ere night
We shall try fortune in a second fight.   *Exeunt.*

Scene Four

[*Another part of the Field*]

*Alarum.   Enter Brutus, Messala, Cato, Lucilius, and
Flavius.*

   Bru. Yet, countrymen, O yet hold up your heads!
   Cato. What bastard doth not?   Who will go with
      me?
I will proclaim my name about the field:
I am the son of Marcus Cato, ho!   4
A foe to tyrants, and my country's friend;
I am the son of Marcus Cato, ho!

96 proper: *individual*   101 fellow: *equal*
104 Thasos: *isle near Thrace*   106 discomfort: *dishearten*
109, 110 three o'clock . . . second fight; *cf. n.*
2 What . . . not: *Who is so base-born as not to do so?*

Enter Soldiers, and fight.

[*Bru.*] And I am Brutus, Marcus Brutus, I;
Brutus, my country's friend; know me for Brutus!
                    [*Exit Brutus, fighting.   Cato is slain.*]
 Lucil. O young and noble Cato, art thou down? 9
Why, now thou diest as bravely as Titinius,
And may'st be honour'd being Cato's son.
 First Sold. Yield, or thou diest.
 Lucil.   Only I yield to die: 12
There is so much, that thou wilt kill me straight:
Kill Brutus, and be honour'd in his death.
 First Sold. We must not.   A noble prisoner!
 Sec. Sold. Room, ho!   Tell Antony, Brutus is
  ta'en. 16
 First Sold. I'll tell the news: here comes the gen-
  eral.

Enter Antony.

Brutus is ta'en, Brutus is ta'en, my lord.
 Ant. Where is he?
 Lucil. Safe, Antony; Brutus is safe enough: 20
I dare assure thee that no enemy
Shall ever take alive the noble Brutus:
The gods defend him from so great a shame!
When you do find him, or alive or dead, 24
He will be found like Brutus, like himself.
 Ant. This is not Brutus, friend; but, I assure you,
A prize no less in worth.   Keep this man safe,
Give him all kindness: I had rather have 28
Such men my friends than enemies.   Go on,
And see whether Brutus be alive or dead;
And bring us word, unto Octavius' tent,
How everything is chanc'd.   *Exeunt.*

7 [Bru.]; *cf. n.*
12 Only . . . die: *I yield only in order that I may die* 13, 14 *Cf. n.*

Scene Five

[Another part of the Field]

Enter Brutus, Dardanius, Clitus, Strato, and
Volumnius.

Bru. Come, poor remains of friends, rest on this
rock.

Cli. Statilius show'd the torch-light; but, my lord,
He came not back: he is or ta'en or slain.

Bru. Sit thee down, Clitus: slaying is the word;   4
It is a deed in fashion. Hark thee, Clitus.

                                  [Whispers.]

Cli. What, I, my lord? No, not for all the world.

Bru. Peace, then: no words.

Cli.   I'll rather kill myself.

Bru. Hark thee, Dardanius.   *[Whispers.]*

Dar.   Shall I do such a deed?   8

Cli. O, Dardanius!

Dar. O, Clitus!

Cli. What ill request did Brutus make to thee?

Dar. To kill him, Clitus. Look, he meditates.

Cli. Now is that noble vessel full of grief,   13
That it runs over even at his eyes.

Bru. Come hither, good Volumnius: list a word.

Vol. What says my lord?

Bru.   Why this, Volumnius: 16
The ghost of Cæsar hath appear'd to me
Two several times by night; at Sardis once,
And this last night here in Philippi fields.
I know my hour is come.

Vol.   Not so, my lord.   20

Bru. Nay, I am sure it is, Volumnius.

1 poor remains of: *few surviving*
2, 3 *Cf. n.*   13 noble vessel: *cf. 2 Tim. 2. 21*

Thou seest the world, Volumnius, how it goes;
Our enemies have beat us to the pit: *Low alarums.*
It is more worthy to leap in ourselves,   24
Than tarry till they push us.   Good Volumnius,
Thou know'st that we two went to school together:
Even for that our love of old, I prithee,
Hold thou my sword-hilts whilst I run on it.   28
  Vol. That's not an office for a friend, my lord.
                      Alarum still.
  Cli. Fly, fly, my lord: there is no tarrying here!
  Bru. Farewell to you; and you; and you, Volum-
    nius.

Strato, thou hast been all this while asleep;   32
Farewell to thee too, Strato.   Countrymen,
My heart doth joy that yet, in all my life,
I found no man but he was true to me.
I shall have glory by this losing day   36
More than Octavius and Mark Antony
By this vile conquest shall attain unto.
So fare you well at once; for Brutus' tongue
Hath almost ended his life's history: 40
Night hangs upon mine eyes; my bones would rest,
That have but labour'd to attain this hour.
           Alarum.   Cry within, 'Fly, fly, fly!'
  Cli. Fly, my lord, fly!
  Bru.   Hence: I will follow.
    [*Exeunt Clitus, Dardanius, and Volumnius.*]
I prithee, Strato, stay thou by thy lord: 44
Thou art a fellow of a good respect;
Thy life hath had some smatch of honour in it:
Hold then my sword, and turn away thy face,

23 pit: *brink of destruction*
39 at once: *once for all; or, all of you*
39, 40 Brutus' . . . history: *Brutus' life will end with this very*
    speech, almost
42 *Cf. Psalm 90. 10*
46 smatch: *smack, flavor*

While I do run upon it. Wilt thou, Strato?   48
  Stra. Give me your hand first: fare you well, my
    lord.
  Bru. Farewell, good Strato.—Cæsar, now be still;
I kill'd not thee with half so good a will.   *Dies.*

Alarum. Retreat. Enter Antony, Octavius, Messala,
Lucilius, and the Army.

  Oct. What man is that?   52
  Mes. My master's man. Strato, where is thy
    master?
  Stra. Free from the bondage you are in, Messala;
The conquerors can but make a fire of him;
For Brutus only overcame himself,   56
And no man else hath honour by his death.
  Lucil. So Brutus should be found. I thank thee,
    Brutus,
That thou hast prov'd Lucilius' saying true.
  Oct. All that serv'd Brutus, I will entertain
    them.   60
Fellow, wilt thou bestow thy time with me?
  Stra. Ay, if Messala will prefer me to you.
  Oct. Do so, good Messala.
  Mes. How died my master, Strato?   64
  Stra. I held the sword, and he did run on it.
  Mes. Octavius, then take him to follow thee
That did the latest service to my master.
  Ant. This was the noblest Roman of them all;   68
All the conspirators save only he
Did that they did in envy of great Cæsar;
He only, in a general honest thought
And common good to all, made one of them.   72

56 only: *alone*   60 entertain: *employ*
61 bestow . . . with: *devote thy time to*
62 prefer: *recommend, transfer*   71, 72 *Cf. n.*

His life was gentle, and the elements
So mix'd in him that Nature might stand up
And say to all world, 'This was a man!'

   Oct. According to his virtue let us use him,   **76**
With all respect and rites of burial.
Within my tent his bones to-night shall lie,
Most like a soldier, order'd honourably.
So, call the field to rest; and let's away   **80**
To part the glories of this happy day.

                               Exeunt omnes.

---

73 gentle: *that of a true gentleman*   elements: *as microcosm, man
was believed to be composed of earth, air, fire, and water, mingled
in due proportions*
76 use: *treat*
79 Most like: *as best befits*   order'd: *arrayed*
80 field: *troops in the field*
81 part: *share*

FINIS.

NOTES

I. i. S. d. *Marullus.* The Folios spell this name incorrectly, 'Murellus.' The emendation, based on Plutarch and other conclusive ancient authorities, is Theobald's. On similar grounds, certain other orthographical vagaries have been corrected in most of the modern editions: e.g., the Folios print 'Calphurnia,' 'Antonio,' 'Claudio,' 'Varrus,' etc. On the other hand, 'Decius Brutus' for 'Decimus' is a genuine confusion of identity which Shakespeare took over from North's Plutarch (see Appendix A).

I. i. 25. *with awl.* The original Folio pointing and spelling of the text will serve to suggest a further pun not obvious in the modern texts: 'I meddle with no Tradesmans matters, nor womens matters; but withal I am indeed Sir, a Surgeon to old shooes.'

I. i. 35. *triumph.* This triumph celebrated Cæsar's defeat of the sons of Pompey at the battle of Munda, in Spain, March 17, B. C. 45, and was the first such recognition of a Roman's victory over any but a foreign foe.—Shakespeare throughout has compressed the historical duration of the play's action considerably, in the interests of dramatic effectiveness: so here he has this triumph coincide with the festival of the Lupercalia, February 15, B. C. 44; in Act III he places the murder, the funeral orations, and the arrival of Octavius all on the same day, whereas in reality some two months elapsed between the earliest and the latest of these events; and in Act V he combines in a single action the two battles of Philippi, whicn really were separated by a three-week interval. See further, for the use of 'Double Time' in this play, the note on II. i. 61, 62.

I. i. 49. *her.* 'Father Tiber' would seem to demand a masculine pronoun, and Rowe accordingly, followed by several other editors, changed 'her' to 'his' in this line and line 51; but Elizabethan usage was less strict than classical, and Shakespeare's laxity was not a special peculiarity of his own.

I. i. 71. *Lupercal.* Ancient Roman festival of purification and expiation, celebrated February 15, and believed to give new life and fruitfulness to fields, flocks, and human beings. After due sacrifices had been offered, the chosen young men, called 'Luperci,' ran around the Palatine hill and struck with their thongs of goatskin those who stood in their way, thus warding off barrenness. These thongs were called 'februa,' from 'februare, to purify'; the day, 'dies februatus'; and the whole month, 'februarius.'

I. ii. 154. *walks.* The famous and spacious paved Roman Ways, such as the 'Via Appia,' 'Via Sacra,' 'Via Flaminia,' etc., are here put for the city itself, by synecdoche. Or, another sound explanation is based on III. ii. 252; 'walks' thus would signify the parks and promenades forming the outlying suburbs of the city. Rowe's emendation, 'walls,' though widely accepted, is unnecessary and prosaic.

I. ii. 165. The punctuation in this line is that of Pope's second edition, and has been generally adopted; but the Folio gives a perfectly plausible reading without emendation: 'I would not so (with love I might entreat you) Be any further moved.'

I. ii. 198. *my name.* A Latin idiom, meaning 'I myself, Cæsar.' For parallels from Virgil, Milton, and the Bible, cf. R. C. Browne's note on *Paradise Lost,* II, 964, in the Clarendon Press edition of *English Poems by John Milton,* 1906.

I. ii. 203. *he hears no music.* Cf. *Merchant of Venice,* V. i. 83-88.

I. ii. 320. *He should not humour me.* 'He,' as is shown by the 'he' in the preceding line and the 'his' in the following, refers to Brutus, not to Cæsar. Cassius then says: 'If I had Brutus' standing with Cæsar and Brutus only mine, Brutus should not (as easily as I mean to beguile him into doing so) talk me into forgoing the advantages afforded by Cæsar's favor.'

I. iii. 60. *cast yourself in wonder.* 'Plunge headlong into, abjectly abandon yourself to, unreasoning wonder.' Cf. 'cast down,' and the etymology of 'abject.' There is no need for emendation, though 'case' has been widely accepted.

I. iii. 65. *Why old men, fools, and children calculate.* This line has occasioned much discussion. Many editors emend it thus: 'Why old men fool, and children calculate,' i.e., 'Why the wise are foolish and the foolish wise.' But against this emendation may be urged the facts that 'old men' are not always 'wise,' in Shakespeare or elsewhere, and that the unaltered text affords an acceptable meaning: 'Why dotards, idiots, and infants so far depart from their ordinary characteristics as to utter the profound truths of divination.'

I. iii. 107-111. 'The idea seems to be that, as men start a huge fire with worthless straws or shavings, so Cæsar is using the degenerate Romans of the time, to set the whole world ablaze with his own glory.' (Hudson.)

I. iii. 126. *Pompey's porch.* A magnificent colonnade or portico surrounding an open area which contained avenues of sycamore trees, fountains, and statues; it was attached to Pompey's theatre (line 152), in the Campus Martius, the first stone theatre to be erected in Rome.

II. i. 15. *Crown him that.* 'Once make him *that*—i.e., once let him become the full-grown adder—by crowning him, and then I realize that we shall be rendering actual a peril (sting) which now is only potential and latent.' Emendations seem unnecessary, though many have been proposed and few editors retain the Folio and Quarto punctuation given in the present text.

II. i. 59. *fourteen.* This is Theobald's generally accepted emendation of the Folio and Quarto reading, 'fifteen.' To Brutus (line 40) it is still the night of the fourteenth. If 'fifteen' days were indeed 'wasted,' i.e., gone, then the ides too would be gone,—which is just what the Soothsayer points out that they are *not* (III. i. 2).

II. i. 61, 62. Literally interpreted, this statement is incredible, if we stop to reflect that a month has passed since I. ii; Brutus then can mean merely 'I have not slept well.' But as a rule we do *not* stop to reflect thus mathematically, and so we have the impression that 'Cassius first did whet' Brutus 'against Cæsar' only a night or two before and that Brutus' sleeplessness has not been superhumanly protracted; for seemingly 'Brought you Cæsar home?' (I. iii. 1) means home from the Lupercal (I. ii), and Casca himself in I. iii is returning from his dinner engagement on the night of the Lupercal (I. ii. 294), so that I. iii apparently follows I. ii without any interval; while II. i apparently follows I. iii with almost equal immediacy, for in their last conversation (on stage: I. ii. 308-312) Brutus and Cassius arranged to meet again at Brutus' home 'to-morrow,' and hence (II. i. 70 ff.) we have their first meeting (on stage) since that time. This device, whereby Shakespeare secures an *impression* of rapid, uninterruptedly continuous action while unobtrusively supplying to *reflection* all needed data for the determination of the actual historical intervals involved, is known as the phenomenon of 'Double Time,' and is well shown further in Acts IV and V of this play. The Short or Dramatic Time-scheme maintains the tension of the passion, while the Long or Historic Time-scheme satisfies the requirements of the analytical reason; but, needless to say, this curious phenomenon is noticeable only in the study, never in the theatre. (Cf. 'Shakespeare's Legerdemain with Time in *Julius Cæsar,*' *Poet Lore,* XI, 1899.)

II. i. 250. *humour.* There were supposed to be four fundamental 'humours' or fluids (from the Latin 'humor,' liquid) in the human body, viz., blood, phlegm, yellow bile, and black bile; and an over-proportion of one of these elements in the system made the disposition predominantly sanguine, phlegmatic, choleric, or melancholy, respectively. So, to the mediæval and renaissance mind, 'humour' might mean literally 'moisture,' as in line 262; or it might account for mental or physical disorder, as in the present line; or it might refer to the more trivial temperamental eccentricity resulting from the fundamental derangement, as in II. ii. 56.

II. ii. 89. *For tinctures, stains, relics, and cognizance.* The generally accepted interpretation explains these terms in the very spirit of Calpurnia's dream, i.e., as the appropriate concomitants of martyrdom; but surely nothing could be further from Cæsar's desire or Decius' intention. Consequently, the gloss attempts to give meanings more in keeping with the manifest purpose of Decius as shown in the rest of his speech, and with the obvious requirements of the situation: i.e., Cæsar's blood is to provide metaphorical living blessings, rather than literal physical souvenirs of death.

II. ii. 128. *That every 'like' is not 'the same.'* The heart of Brutus grieves to realize that specious resemblance is not genuine identity; that appearances (of friendship, as in the amicable ceremony of taking wine together) are deceptive; that the conspirators, who seem 'like friends' (line 127), are so far from being truly Cæsar's friends that they are on the very point of putting him to death.

III. i. S. d. *Before the Capitol.* In the original texts there is no stage direction in this scene before 'They stab Cæsar,' at line 76, other than the opening direction: 'Flourish. Enter Cæsar, Brutus,' and the rest. Yet lines 11, 12 show that the action takes place outdoors; while lines 31, 79, 115, 119, etc., as well as the familiar tradition and all pictorial representations, show that the murder takes place indoors. Of course, there was no difficulty here on the Elizabethan stage: the action of the first 12 lines would take place on the fore-stage, and then Cæsar would withdraw and seat himself on the dais or inner stage at the rear, with the Senators grouped about him and the approaching conspirators between him and the audience. Except for the standardization of the text established by the almost unbroken succession of editors who have left this dilemma unamended, there would seem to be no reason why the procedure followed in the precisely similar dilemma in IV. ii and iii should not be adopted here: there the action outside Brutus' tent is assigned to a brief Scene Two, while the action inside the tent is very properly assigned to a long separate scene, Scene Three. It must be remembered that *all* the Scene-divisions in this play have had to be determined by modern editors, there being nothing but Act-divisions in the Folios after the initial 'Scæna Prima.'

Capitol. Shakespeare placed the killing of Cæsar in the Capitol on account of the established popular and literary tradition to that effect; cf., e.g., Chaucer, *The Monkes Tale,* 713-718, and *Hamlet, III.* ii. 109-112. In reality Cæsar was assassinated in the Curia Pompeiana, a great hall adjoining the portico of Pompey's theatre (cf. note on I. iii. 126). This Curia was used for meetings of the Senate and was destroyed in the grief and rage over Cæsar's death, but the colossal statue of Pompey which it had contained (cf. line 115) was saved.

III. i. 47, 48. *Know, Cæsar doth not wrong.* Ben Jonson quoted in his *Discoveries,* first printed in 1641, an alternative version of this line: 'Cæsar did never wrong but with just cause.' Jonson ridiculed this sentence as an 'Irish bull'—unjustly: for 'wrong' means not only 'error, mistake,' but also 'harm, injury' (as in line 242 in this very scene). Some few editors have incorporated Jonson's version of this line in the text, following it up with 'Nor without cause will he be satisfied,' on the hypothesis that Jonson was quoting either an early Quarto version which has since disappeared, or at least the acting version current in Shakespeare's lifetime which was unwarrantably changed by the editors of the First Folio.

III. i. 59. *If I could pray to move, prayers would move me.* 'If I were as weak as you are, and in the position of looking up to someone more powerful than myself and entreating him to change his mind, why then I should perhaps be weak enough likewise to change my own mind on account of mere empty entreaties; but happily I am as far above one alternative as the other, for,' etc.

III. i. 174. This line has given the commentators much trouble, and many emendations have been proposed for the puzzling phrase 'in strength of malice'— such as 'exempt from malice,' 'in strength of amity,' etc. If the Folio reading is to be preserved unchanged, the word 'malice' must clearly be emptied of all its usual meaning, for Brutus could never have applied such a term to any action by the conspirators after his overwhelming repudiation of 'envy' and similar emotions in II. i. 162-183; and the word 'malice,' free from its usual sinister implications, apparently does occur elsewhere in Shakespeare (e.g., *Macbeth,* III. ii. 14, 25, and perhaps *John,* II. i. 251), and is recognized by the Oxford Dictionary, in the sense of 'power, capacity.' Cf. the note, in this edition, on *Macbeth,* III. ii. 14. But even so, that interpretation gives a very inferior meaning to the phrase now under discussion, little better than tautology and not very appropriate to the spirit of the context. The present editor therefore ventures to suggest as an emendation here 'instranged' (of the use of which *N. E. D.* gives an example dated 1586), a variant of 'enstranged' (*N. E. D.*: Caxton, 1483), meaning 'estranged, far removed, deprived,' etc. This rare word, 'instranged,' unfamiliar to the compositor's eye or ear, would be very naturally sophisticated into 'in strength,' while it supplies exactly the sense needed in the passage; viz., 'Our arms free from malice, and our hearts of brothers' temper, do receive you in,' etc.

III. i. 273. *dogs of war.* Most editors explain the 'dogs' literally and specifically as 'fire, sword, and famine,' on the strength of *Henry V,* I. Prologue 8. But why should not the phrase be merely a general poetic metaphor—on the analogy of 'dove of peace'—designed to suggest all the nameless horrors that result when the destructive energies of ruthless warfare are unpent?

III. ii. 178. *That day he overcame the Nervii.* It was in the summer of 57 B. C. that this most warlike of Belgic tribes was defeated, in the battle of the Sambre. The Nervii made a successful surprise attack, and only Cæsar's personal bravery saved the day. Cf. *De Bello Gallico,* II. 15-28. This victory is prominently featured in North's Plutarch (see Appendix A), and was celebrated at Rome with unprecedented thanksgivings and rejoicings.

III. ii. 247. *drachmas.* These were Greek silver coins, of a value impossible to compute accurately in terms of modern currency. In purchasing power the bequest would perhaps be equivalent to-day to something over $100 per citizen.

III. ii. 254. *On this side Tiber.* The gardens lay across the Tiber from the Forum in which Antony was speaking, but 'on this side' from the French and English standpoint of Amyot and North—whom Shakespeare too literally follows.

IV. i. 37. *one that feeds On objects, arts, and imitations Which, out of use and stal'd by other men, Begin his fashion.* The Folio text here is at least as satisfactory as any emendation, if the punctuation makes it evident that the disputed 'objects, arts, and imitations' are immediately defined by the restrictive relative clause that follows. Despite his unbridled passions, Antony is eminently a practical politician,—as witness the form of Cassius' bribe offered to him after Brutus' futile expression of idealism (III. i. 177, 178); and witness also his masterly manipulation of the conspirators and the mob, in III. i and III. ii. He scorns Lepidus then for so lacking personality, initiative, shrewdness, and judgment that he takes even the superficial embellishments of life at second hand, unable to distinguish between the true values and the sham. (Staunton's emendation would substitute 'abjects,' meaning 'discarded scraps,' and 'orts,' meaning 'leavings.')

IV. i. 48, 49. *we are at the stake, And bay'd about with many enemies.* This refers to the very popular but very brutal Elizabethan amusement of bear-baiting, wherein the bear was chained to a stake in the center of the 'bear-garden' or arena (the best-known one was situated close by the Globe Theatre) and attacked by a number of dogs.

IV. iii. S. d. For the 'Enter' of modern editions
the Folios and Quartos have 'Manet' or 'Manent.'
I.e., as explained in the note on III. i. S. d., no new
scene was necessary here on the Elizabethan stage:
the armies marched off and Brutus and Cassius simply
'remained' in conference, but the locality none the
less was supposed to shift to the inside of Brutus'
tent.

IV. iii. 20, 21. *What villain touch'd his body, that
did stab, And not for justice?* 'What one of the conspirators was such a villain that he stabbed Cæsar
from any other motive than for justice's sake?'
Brutus means, of course, to imply that there was
none such then, and they must be doubly careful to
avoid giving ground for any such imputation now.

IV. iii. 25, 26. The infinite spiritual extent of true
honor is contrasted with the petty material extent of
a handful of money.

IV. iii. 28. *Brutus, bay not me.* 'Bay' (Theobald's widely accepted emendation of the Folio reading 'bait') is a savage and threatening quibble on
Cassius' part: 'Don't bark at me, Brutus, and don't
bring me to bay either (cf. note on IV. i. 48, 49),
hedging me in with snarling accusations and goading
me on with taunts, or I'll turn on you and then it will
be the worse for you.' 'Bait' can be given almost the
same interpretation, with reference to bear-baiting,
but misses the neat repartee in the repeated 'bay.'

IV. iii. 101. *Pluto's.* As god of the infernal
regions, Pluto might well be supposed to command
great wealth. As Milton says, 'Let none admire That
riches grow in Hell; that soil may best Deserve the
precious banc.' Many editors, however, prefer to
follow Pope in reading 'Plutus',' the god of riches.
Confusion between the two occurred in classical times
as well as in Elizabethan.

IV. iii. 109-112. This badly mixed metaphor can

be straightened out if we punctuate 'lamb,—' and interpret 'That' as 'With one that, with a man who,' thus: 'O Cassius, you are associated with a mere lamb,—with a man whose anger is as negative and latent as the fire in a flint, which needs a hard blow before showing any flame at all and even then yields only a momentary spark.'

IV. iii. 152. *grief.* The grammatical construction breaks down here (though the sense is clear enough), unless we (1) construe 'grief' with 'impatient of' in the preceding line, thus: 'Unable to endure my absence and her own sorrow over Antony's success'; or (2) read 'grieved' for 'grief,' thus: 'Impatient and grieved, in this situation she fell distract,' etc.

IV. iii. 183. *Nothing, Messala.* Various more or less plausible attempts have been made to defend Brutus from this most unpleasant appearance of deceiving Messala in order to win applause for his fortitude under affliction, but the best way out of the difficulty lies in accepting the suggestion of J. Resch that two alternative versions of Brutus' stoical conduct have been accidentally taken over into the Folio text from the MS. or prompt-book copy.

V. i. 53. *three-and-thirty.* According to North's Plutarch the number of Cæsar's wounds was three-and-twenty, and several editors have followed Theobald in making the somewhat meticulous correction.

V. i. 111-115. In these lines Brutus has been charged by many critics with flatly contradicting his declaration against suicide in lines 101-108; but the inconsistency disappears if the significance of lines 113, 114 be grasped (by a proper interpretation of 'Must') as merely restating the stoical fatalism of lines 106-108, for Brutus really says simply this: 'No, Cassius, you are an Epicurean and do not understand, and I cannot take the time now to explain

things to you. No, I bear too great a mind ever to
go bound to Rome: *but (my mere human mind does
not have to settle this point, for) this same day Must
(i.e., will certainly) end that work the ides of March
begun.'* I.e., 'I do not have to alter my resolution
against suicide for Fate will decide, and to-day either
we shall kill Cæsar's usurping successors as we killed
Cæsar himself, or we shall ourselves die fighting and
thus even the score, pay the reckoning, for Cæsar's
death.' This, as Hunter points out, is Brutus' expression of mere speculative theory: if, like Hamlet, he
does not live up to his professed principles and ab-
stract resolution when the actual test comes, that is
but part of his tragic failure.

V. iii. 109, 110. The 'second fight' really took
place twenty days later. Cf. note on I. i. 35.

V. iv. 7. No speaker's name precedes this speech
in the Folios, and it is accordingly assigned to Brutus
on the strength of modern editorial authority only.
Some editors, however, would assign it to Lucilius,
in order to prepare the audience for his assumption
of the rôle of Brutus in lines 12-14 below.

V. iv. 13, 14. Many editors supply a stage direction [*Offering money*] to explain 'There is so much';
but surely there would be little sense in offering to
give part, where all would naturally fall to his slayer.
So Lucilius presumably meant simply this: 'I yield
only to ensure dying at once: and there is so much
reason for my death and so much advantage in it
for you that you will doubtless kill me immediately;
for you have only to kill me, i.e., Brutus, in order to
win great honor and rewards.'

V. v. 2, 3. This passage is somewhat obscure
without its original context in North's Plutarch:
'Brutus thought that there was no great number of
men slain in battle: and to know the truth of it, there
was one called Statilius, that promised to go through

his enemies, for otherwise it was impossible to go see
their camp: and from thence, if all were well, that
he would lift up a torch-light in the air, and then
return again with speed to him.'—*Life of Brutus.*

V. v. 71, 72. 'He consented to join them only on
impersonal principles of honor and in the hope of
promoting the welfare of all.'

APPENDIX A

SOURCES OF THE PLAY

There were, of course, earlier plays in Elizabethan England on the subject of Cæsar's career (Henslowe's Diary attests their popularity in the 1590's) and they may well have influenced Shakespeare's work. For a careful study of these possibilities, see H. M. Ayres' 'Shakespeare's *Julius Cæsar* in the Light of Some Other Versions' (Pub. Mod. Lang. Assoc. of America, 1910). Dr. A. Boecker also has put forward an elaborate effort to establish Shakespeare's indebtedness to Orlando Pescetti's 'Il Cesare,' a tragedy running to nearly four thousand lines of verse and published in Verona in 1594, 2d ed. 1604 ('A Probable Italian Source of Shakespeare's *Julius Cæsar*,' N. Y. Univ. Dissertation, 1913). But after all due allowances have been made for this sort of influence, and for the less important possibility of indebtedness to classic authors such as Appian, it still remains true that the great source of the play is 'The Lives of the Noble Grecians and Romanes, Compared together by that grave learned Philosopher and Historiographer, Plutarke of Chæronea: Translated out of Greeke into French by Iames Amyot . . . and out of French into Englishe, by *Thomas North*. Imprinted at London . . . 1579,' 2d ed. 1595, 3d ed. 1603. To this famous and splendid monument of Elizabethan prose Shakespeare owes the whole action or plot of the play, the separate incidents, many personal details of characterization, some few errors in fact, and occasional verbal suggestions: but his supreme skill in selecting, rejecting, combining, and arranging historical material has rarely been shown

to better advantage than in his handling of the three
'Lives' on which he drew,—those, namely, of Cæsar,
Brutus, and Antony; while his power of poetic and
dramatic transformation will appear upon comparing
Act III, Scene i with the following typical passage
from North:

'For these things, they may seem to come by
chance: but the place where the murther was pre-
pared, and where the Senate were assembled, and
where also there stood up an image of *Pompey* dedi-
cated by him selfe amongest other ornaments which
he gave unto the Theater: all these were manifest
proofes, that it was the ordinaunce of some god that
made this treason to be executed, specially in that
very place. It is also reported that Cassius (though
otherwise hee did favour the doctrine of *Epicurus*)
beholding the image of *Pompey,* before they entred
into the action of their traiterous enterprise; hee did
softly call uppon it to aide him. But the instant
danger of the present time, taking away his former
reason, did sodainly put him into a furious passion,
and made him like a man halfe besides him selfe.
Now *Antonius,* that was a faithfull friend to *Cæsar,*
and a valiant man besides of his handes, him *Decius
Brutus Albinus* entertained out of the Senate house,
having begunne a long tale of set purpose. So *Cæsar*
comming into the house, all the Senate stood up on
their feete to doe him honor. The part of Brutus
company and confederates stoode round about Cæsars
chayre, and part of them also came towardes him, as
though they made sute with *Metellus Cimber,* to call
home his brother againe from banishment: and thus
prosecuting still their sute, they followed *Cæsar,* till
hee was set in his chaire. Who, denying their petitions, and being offended with them one after an
other, because the more they were denied the more
they pressed uppon him, and were the earnester with

him: *Metellus* at length, taking his gowne with both
his hands, pulled it over his necke, which was the
signe given the confederats to set uppon him.   Then
Casca, behinde him, strake him in the necke with his
sword, howbeit the wound was not great nor mortall,
because it seemed the feare of such a devilish attempt
did amaze him and take his strength from him, that
he killed him not at the first blow.   But *Cæsar* turning straight unto him, caught hold of his sword, and
held it hard: & they both cried out, *Cæsar* in Latin:
O vile traitor *Casca,* what doest thou?   And *Casca* in
Greeke to his brother, brother, helpe mee.   At the
beginning of this stur, they that were present, not
knowing of the conspiracy, were so amazed with the
horrible sight they saw: they had no power to flie,
neither to helpe him, not so much, as once to make
an outcry.   They on the other side that had conspired
his death compassed him in on everie side with their
swords drawen in their hands, that *Cæsar* turned him
no where but hee was stricken at by some, and still
had naked swords in his face, and was hacked and
mangled among them, as a wilde beast taken of
hunters.   For it was agreede among them, that every
man should give him a wound, because all their parts
should be in this murther: and then *Brutus* gave him
one. . . . Men report also, that *Cæsar* did still de-
fende him selfe against the rest, running every way
with his body: but when he saw *Brutus* with his
sword drawen in his hand, then he pulled his gowne
over his head, and made no more resistaunce, and was
driven either casually, or purposedly, by the counsell
of the conspirators, against the base whereupon Pompeys image stoode, which ran all of a goare bloud till
he was slain.   Thus it seemed that the image tooke
just revenge of Pompeys enemy, being throwen downe
on the ground at his feete, and yeelding up his ghost
there, for the number of wounds he had upon him.

For it is reported, that he had three and twenty wounds upon his body: and divers of the conspirators did hurt themselves, striking one body with so many blowes. When *Cæsar* was slaine, the Senate (though *Brutus* stood in the middest amongst them, as though he would have saied somewhat touching this fact) presently ran out of the house, and flying, filled all the city with marvellous feare and tumult.' (From 'The Life of Julius Cæsar,' North's 2d ed., 1595, as quoted by Furness, pp. 300, 301.)

APPENDIX B

The History of the Play

The earliest extant version of Shakespeare's *Julius Cæsar* is that found in the famous First Folio collected edition of his plays, published in 1623, which therefore necessarily forms the basis of all modern texts; for the only known Quarto editions belong to the late Restoration period and so, unfortunately, have little critical value for the solution of the problems presented by the original text. It seems fairly certain now that *Julius Cæsar* was written and first produced in 1599, for on the twenty-first of September in that year a German traveller witnessed a performance of what was presumably Shakespeare's play at the Globe Theatre (cf. 'Londoner Theater und Schauspiele im Jahre 1599,' G. Binz, *Anglia,* xxii, 456, 1899). The next performance that we can date seems to have taken place at court early in 1613, the next at St. James', January 31, 1636-7, and the next at the Cockpit, November 13, 1638; but that the popularity of the play was far greater than these meagre records suggest is attested by various kinds of evidence, from Henslowe's effort to capitalize its success

by producing a rival Cæsar play, in 1602, to Digges'
striking tribute prefixed to the First Folio.[1]

After the Restoration, *Julius Cæsar* is one of the
three Shakespearean dramas listed by Downes ('Ros-
cius Anglicanus,' 1708) among the 'Principal Old
Stock Plays' given by Killigrew's company in the
1660's. Charles Hart (d. 1683), grandson of Shakespeare's sister Joan, was the great Brutus of this
period, and was succeeded by the famous Thomas
Betterton (1635 ?-1710); it is Betterton's cast (see
the frontispiece to the present volume) that is given
in the six Quarto editions published between 1684 and
1691, evidently printed as playgoers' guides (cf.
'Quarto Editions of *Julius Cæsar,*' by Miss H. C.
Bartlett, *The Library,* 1913).

It is worthy of note that *Julius Cæsar* is one of
the few Shakespearean plays that escaped mutilation
at the hands of so-called adapters or revisers, during
the seventeenth and eighteenth centuries, for the
abortive efforts in 1719 and 1722 had no success or
significance (cf. F. W. Kilbourne's 'Alterations and
Adaptations of Shakespeare,' Boston, 1906). A
plausible sketch by Miss C. Porter ('How Shakespeare Set and Struck the Scene for *Julius Cæsar* in
1599,' *Mod. Lang. Notes,* 1916) gives a pleasant
glimpse into Elizabethan stage procedure, and William Winter's 'Shakespeare on the Stage' (Second
Series, 1915) supplies many illuminating hints about
the stage 'business' in succeeding and modern pro-
ductions; while Brander Matthews ('Shaksperian
Stage Traditions' in 'Shaksperian Studies,' Columbia
Univ. Press, 1916) gives a spirited picture of the
Meiningen company's remarkable presentation of the
Forum scene and Antony's oration.

[1] 'The Shakspere Allusion-Book' lists ten (should be
eleven ? Digges, p. 318, is not indexed) references to *Julius
Cæsar* down to 1649, and twenty-five more between 1650
and 1700.

In the early eighteenth century Robert Wilks (1665 ?-1732), the friend of Farquhar, was a brilliant Antony, while Barton Booth (1681-1733) and James Quin (1693-1766) excelled as Brutus. Garrick never acted in *Julius Cæsar*, but his rival, Spranger Barry (1719-1777), was a most moving Antony. The famous Peg Woffington (1714 ?-1760) appeared as Portia in several performances about 1750, but because the part is such a minor one it has not been taken by many great actresses since then. Coming down to the nineteenth century, we find all the greatest actors appearing in the play. The Kembles and Young, Macready and Davenport, Wallack, Charles Kean, J. B. Booth, Samuel Phelps, and Beerbohm Tree have all presented one or more of the four leading rôles. The first American performance was given at Charleston, S. C., April 20, 1774. Edwin Forrest and John Edward McCullough are also associated with the play, as are Tyrone Power, William Faversham, and Robert Bruce Mantell in our own time; but the crowning achievement in America's production of *Julius Cæsar* will always be the magnificent double triumph of Edwin Booth and Lawrence Barrett, in the '60's, '70's, and '80's, with honorable mention, perhaps, of Richard Mansfield's sombre portrayal of Brutus' tragic loneliness, beginning October 14, 1902. It is not easy nowadays to realize the power and effectiveness attributed by tradition to these great players of the past, but fortunately it is still possible to gain some impression of Edwin Booth's thrilling personal magnetism and manifest genius from the inspired portrait by John S. Sargent in the Players' Club, New York City.

APPENDIX C

The Text of the Present Edition

The text of the present volume is, by permission of the Oxford University Press, that of the Oxford Shakespeare, edited by the late W. J. Craig, except for the following deviations:

1. The stage directions of the Folio have been restored as far as possible, with necessary modern additions in square brackets.

2. The punctuation, especially in the use of exclamation points, has been modernized, and the spelling of Calpurnia brought into conformity with current usage.

3. The only significant verbal departures—usually in the direction of a return to the Folio—are listed below, the readings adopted in the present text being placed before the colon while Craig's readings follow it; and Folio authority is given wherever involved:

I. i. 65	whether: whe'r (F where)
ii. 154	walks F: walls
iii. 96	these F: those
II. i. 72	moe F: more
275	you are F: are you
283	or F: of
ii. 76	statue F: statua
III. i. 31	*Cæs.* F: *Casca*
206	lethe (F1 Lethee F4 Lethe): leth
209	stricken F2, 3, 4: strucken (F1 stroken)
ii. S. d. et pas.	*Plebeians* F: *Citizens*
193	statue F: statua
IV. i. 37	objects, arts F: abject orts
iii. 13	speaks (speakes F): speak
101	Pluto's F: Plutus'
V. iii. 61	to night F: to-night
97	whether: whe'r (F where)
104	Thasos: Thassos (F Tharsus)
iv. 18	Brutus is ta'en, Brutus is ta'en, my Lord F: Brutus is ta'en, my lord
30	whether: whe'r (F where)

APPENDIX D

Thomas Rymer: *A Short View of Tragedy . . . with some Reflections on Shakespear.* London, 1692-3. (Chapter viii begins with some twelve pages devoted to crude ridicule of *Julius Cæsar.*)

John Dennis: *On the Genius and Writings of Shakespeare.* London, 1711. (Reprinted in D. Nichol Smith's Eighteenth Century Essays on Shakespeare. Glasgow, 1903. Early appreciation of the Roman plays, disgruntled by pseudo-classical bias.)

William Hazlitt: *Characters of Shakespear's Plays.* London, 1817. (Reprinted in 'Everyman's Library.' Standard criticism.)

Samuel Taylor Coleridge: *Lectures and Notes on Shakespeare and Other English Poets.* London, v. d. (Reprinted in 'Everyman's Library,' and in Bohn's Libraries. A landmark in modern literary criticism of Shakespeare.)

Henry Norman Hudson: *Lectures on Shakespeare.* New York, 1848. (Very full and sympathetic interpretations of character and action.)

George L. Craik: *The English of Shakespeare; illustrated in A Philological Commentary on his Julius Cæsar.* Revised ed. by W. J. Rolfe. Boston, 1867. (The most detailed commentary on the text of the play.)

Richard G. Moulton: *Shakespeare as a Dramatic Artist.* Oxford, 1885. (Contains some interesting theories of dramatic construction, with two chapters analyzing *Julius Cæsar.*)

Frederick S. Boas: *Shakspere and his Predecessors.* New York, 1896. (A useful general history, with a noticeably good treatment of *Julius Cæsar* among the discussions of the separate plays.)

Thomas R. Lounsbury: *Shakespeare and Voltaire.* New York, 1902. (A rather prolix study of pseudo-classicism's opposition to Shakespeare, with a searching discussion of Voltaire's revamping of *Julius Cæsar.*)

C. F. Tucker Brooke: *Shakespeare's Plutarch. Vol. I: containing The Main Sources of Julius Cæsar.* London, 1909. (A very convenient and thorough edition of North for the student's purposes.)

M. W. MacCallum: *Shakespeare's Roman Plays and their Background.* London, 1910. (An elaborate and comprehensive work.)

W. F. P. Stockley: *Reading Julius Cæsar.* Dublin, n. d. (By no means first-class in quality, but offering many helpful suggestions to the elementary-school teacher.)

A. DeV. Tassin: *Julius Cæsar,* in *Shaksperian Studies by Members of the Department of English . . . in Columbia University.* New York, 1916. (A fine piece of appreciative criticism, though one may fail to concur in all its views.)

H. H. Furness, Jr.: *A New Variorum Edition of Shakespeare.* Vol. XVII: *Julius Cæsar.* Philadelphia, 1913. (For the faults of this volume, see the present writer's article in *Journal of English and Germanic Philology,* 1919.)

INDEX OF WORDS GLOSSED

(Figures in full-faced type refer to page-numbers)

bloody sign of battle: 84 (V. i. 14)

bold: 26 (II. i. 86)

bootless: 46 (III. i. 75)

bosoms: 83 (V. i. 7)

bound in: 79 (IV. iii. 220)

brav'd: 74 (IV. iii. 95)

break with: 28 (II. i. 150)

brook'd: 10 (I. ii. 158)

brought: 16 (I. iii. 1)

Brutus (Lucius Junius): 10 (I. ii. 158)

Brutus' . . . history: 96 (V. v. 39, 40)

budge: 72 (IV. iii. 44)

but I will do so: 84 (V. i. 20)

by Cæsar: 49 (III. i. 162)

by him: 30 (II. i. 218)

by this: 20 (I. iii. 125)

by . . . whereof: 6 (I. ii. 49)

by your leave, gods: 92 (V. iii. 89)

by your pardon: 52 (III. i. 235)

Cæsar doth not wrong: 45 (III. i. 47)

calculate: 18 (I. iii. 65)

call in question: 77 (IV. iii. 164)

Capitol: 43 (III. i. S. d.)

carrion men (rotting corpses): 53 (III. i. 275)

carrions (wretches): 27 (II. i. 130)

cast . . . in: 18 (I. iii. 60)

Cato: 33 (II. i. 295); 87 (V. i. 102)

cautelous: 27 (II. i. 129)

ceremonies: 3 (I. i. 69)

change: 91 (V. iii. 51)

charactery: 34 (II. i. 308)

charm: 32 (II. i. 271)

check'd: 74 (IV. iii. 96)

chew: 10 (I. ii. 170)

chopped: 13 (I. ii. 245)

clean from the purpose: 17 (I. iii. 35)

climate: 17 (I. iii. 32)

close: 50 (III. i. 202)

closet: 23 (II. i. 35)

cobbler: 1 (I. i. 11)

cognizance: 38 (II. ii. 89)

cold demeanour: 88 (V. ii. 4)

Colossus: 9 (I. ii. 135)

colour: 23 (II. i. 29)

combin'd: 67 (IV. i. 43)

common pulpits: 46 (III. i. 80)

commons (plebeians): 59 (III. ii. 136)

commons (pasture): 67 (IV. i. 27)

companion: 76 (IV. iii. 137)

complexion . . . element: 20 (I. iii. 128)

conceited: 22 (I. iii. 162)

condemn'd to have: 71 (IV. iii. 10)

conference: 11 (I. ii. 187)

confidence: 37 (II. ii. 49)

confines: 53 (III. i. 272)

consorted: 87 (V. i. 83)

constant: 44 (III. i. 22)

construe (explain): 34 (II. i. 307)

construe (read meaning into): 6 (I. ii. 45)

coronets: 12 (I. ii. 238)

corse: 50 (III. i. 199)

couchings: 44 (III. i. 36)

countenance: 22 (I. iii. 159)

courtesies: 44 (III. i. 36)

covert: 68 (IV. iii. 46)

coward: 89 (V. iii. 4)

coward lips . . . colour: 8 (I. ii. 122)

crown him that: 23 (II. i. 15)

cull out: 3 (I. i. 53)

curtsies: 45 (III. i. 43)

full of . . . honour: **68** (IV.
    ii. 12)

gamesome: **5** (I. ii. 28)
general: **22** (II. i. 12)
general coffers: **57** (III. ii.
    95)
genius: **24** (II. i. 66)
gentle: **98** (V. v. 73)
gently: **69** (IV. ii. 31)
get the start of: **9** (I. ii.
    130)
give . . . accidental: **76** (IV.
    iii. 145)
give the word: **68** (IV. ii. 2)
glasses: **30** (II. i. 205)
go to: **71** (IV. iii. 32)
good cheer: **46** (III. i. 89)
good regard: **51** (III. i. 224)
great flood: **9** (I. ii. 151)
grief: **76** (IV. iii. 152)
griefs (grievances): **20** (I.
    iii. 118)
growing on: **26** (II. i. 107)
guilty . . . bastardy: **27** (II.
    i. 138)

had his eyes: **6** (I. ii. 62)
hart: **50** (III. i. 204)
have . . . health: **72** (IV. iii.
    36)
havoc: **53** (III. i. 273)
he hears no music: **11** (I. ii.
    203)
he should not humour me:
    15 (I. ii. 320)
hearts of controversy: **8** (I.
    ii. 109)
held Epicurus strong: **86**
    (V. i. 77)
her: **3** (I. i. 49)
hie: **21** (I. iii. 150)
high-sighted: **27** (II. i. 118)
hinds: **20** (I. iii. 106)
his: **8** (I. ii. 124)
hold, my hand: **20** (I. iii.
    117)

hold thee (wait): **92** (V. iii.
    85)
holds on: **46** (III. i. 69)
holes: **30** (II. i. 205)
hollow: **69** (IV. ii. 23)
honours this corruption: **71**
    (IV. iii. 15)
hot at hand: **69** (IV. ii. 23)
how ill . . . burns: **82** (IV.
    iii. 274)
however: **15** (I. ii. 304)
humour (disposition): **30**
    (II. i. 210)
humour (whim): **37** (II. ii.
    56)
hurtled: **36** (II. ii. 22)
Hybla: **85** (V. i. 34)

ides of March: **5** (I. ii. 18)
imitations: **67** (IV. i. 37)
impatient of: **76** (IV. iii.
    151)
improve: **28** (II. i. 159)
in a general honest thought,
    etc.: **97** (V. v. 71, 72)
in his own change: **68** (IV.
    ii. 7)
in . . . limitation: **33** (II. i.
    283)
in our black . . . proscrip-
    tion: **66** (IV. i. 17)
in respect of: **1** (I. i. 10)
in . . . speed: **4** (I. ii. 6)
in your bad strokes: **84** (V.
    i. 30)
incorporate: **21** (I. iii. 135)
indifferently: **7** (I. ii. 87)
indirection: **73** (IV. iii. 75)
ingrafted: **29** (II. i. 184)
insuppressive: **27** (II. i. 134)
is run his compass: **90** (V.
    iii. 25)
is to: **29** (II. i. 187)
issue: **54** (III. i. 294)
it shall have scope: **74** (IV.
    iii. 107)

jades: 69 (IV. ii. 26)
jealous (doubtful): 10 (I. ii. 161)
jealous on (suspicious of): 7 (I. ii. 71)
jigging: 76 (IV. iii. 136)
just: 6 (I. ii. 54)

kerchief: 34 (II. i. 315)
knave: 80 (IV. iii. 240)
knot: 47 (III. i. 117)
know his humour: 76 (IV. iii. 135)

labour'd . . . hour: 96 (V. v. 42)
law of children: 44 (III. i. 39)
leaden: 81 (IV. iii. 267)
learn'd . . . rote: 74 (IV. iii. 97)
let blood: 49 (III. i. 152)
let slip: 53 (III. i. 273)
lethe: 51 (III. i. 206)
liable: 39 (II. ii. 104)
light: 90 (V. iii. 31)
like (likely): 13 (I. ii. 255)
'like' is not 'the same': 40 (II. ii. 128)
listen: 67 (IV. i. 41)
live (if I live): 49 (III. i. 159)
lodge to-night: 76 (IV. iii. 139)
lost . . . bloods: 9 (I. ii. 150)
lottery: 27 (II. i. 119)
lover: 40 (II. iii. 9)
low-crooked: 45 (III. i. 43)
Lupercal: 3 (I. i. 71)

mace: 81 (IV. iii. 267)
made: 67 (IV. i. 44)
make conditions: 71 (IV. iii. 32)
make forth: 84 (V. i. 25)
make head: 67 (IV. i. 42)
malice: 49 (III. i. 174)

mark of favour: 25 (II. i. 76)
marry: 12 (I. ii. 228)
mart: 71 (IV. iii. 11)
Marullus: 1 (I. i. S. d.)
me (expletive): 13 (I. ii. 267)
mean: 49 (III. i. 161)
mechanical: 1 (I. i. 3)
meet: 10 (I. ii. 169)
melancholy's child: 91 (V. iii. 67)
merely: 6 (I. ii. 39)
mine own: 89 (V. iii. 2)
mistrust . . . success: 91 (V. iii. 65)
mock: 38 (II. ii. 96)
modesty: 51 (III. i. 213)
moe: 25 (II. i. 72)
monstrous state: 18 (I. iii. 71)
more (else): 16 (I. iii. 14)
mortal instruments: 24 (II. i. 66)
mortified: 34 (II. i. 324)
most like: 98 (V. v. 79)
motion: 24 (II. i. 64)
mov'd: 10 (I. ii. 166)
much: 81 (IV. iii. 254)
murderous: 81 (IV. iii. 266)
my name: 11 (I. ii. 198)

napkins: 59 (III. ii. 139)
native: 25 (II. i. 83)
naughty: 1 (I. i. 16)
neat's leather: 2 (I. i. 28)
new-added: 79 (IV. iii. 208)
nice: 71 (IV. iii. 8)
niggard . . . rest: 79 (IV. iii. 227)
night-gown: 35 (II. ii. S. d.)
noble vessel: 95 (V. v. 13)
none so poor: 59 (III. ii. 126)
noted: 70 (IV. iii. 2)

nothing (not at all): **10** (I. ii. 161)

nothing, Messala: **78** (IV. iii. 183)

objects: **67** (IV. i. 37)

observe: **72** (IV. iii. 45)

occupation: **14** (I. ii. 269)

o'er-watch'd: **80** (IV. iii. 240)

of (in): **28** (II. i. 157)

of . . . difference: **6** (I. ii. 40)

old Cassius still: **86** (V. i. 63)

omitted: **79** (IV. iii. 219)

on (being on): **25** (II. i. 83)

on the Lupercal: **58** (III. ii. 101)

once: **78** (IV. iii. 190)

only (alone): **97** (V. v. 56)

only I yield to die: **94** (V. iv. 12)

ope: **13** (I. ii. 267)

or . . . or: **27** (II. i. 135)

orchard: **22** (II. i. S. d.)

order: **51** (III. i. 230)

order of the course: **5** (I. ii. 25)

order'd: **98** (V. v. 79)

ordinance: **18** (I. iii. 66)

ordinary: **7** (I. ii. 73)

our deeds are done: **91** (V. iii. 64)

out (of temper): **2** (I. i. 17)

out of the teeth: **40** (II. iii. 14)

painted: **45** (III. i. 63)

palter: **27** (II. i. 126)

parley: **84** (V. i. 21)

part: **98** (V. v. 81)

part the numbers: **54** (III. ii. 4)

Parthia: **90** (V. iii. 37)

passion: **53** (III. i. 283)

path: **25** (II. i. 83)

peevish: **86** (V. i. 61)

phantasma: **24** (II. i. 65)

physical: **32** (II. i. 261)

pit: **96** (V. v. 23)

pitch: **4** (I. i. 77)

pleasures: **63** (III. ii. 255)

Pluto's: **74** (IV. iii. 101)

point upon: **17** (I. iii. 32)

Pompey's basis: **47** (III. i. 115)

Pompey's blood: **3** (I. i. 55)

Pompey's porch: **20** (I. iii. 126)

poor remains of: **95** (V. v. 1)

posture: **85** (V. i. 33)

powers: **67** (IV. i. 42)

practice: **71** (IV. iii. 31)

prætor's chair: **21** (I. iii. 143)

pray to move: **45** (III. i. 59)

praying on his side: **70** (IV. iii. 4)

prefer (offer): **44** (III. i. 28)

prefer (recommend): **97** (V. v. 62)

pre-ordinance: **44** (III. i. 38)

present: **35** (II. ii. 5)

press: **38** (II. ii. 88)

prevent: **23** (II. i. 28)

prevention: **25** (II. i. 85)

prick'd in number: **51** (III. i. 216)

proceeding: **39** (II. ii. 103)

produce: **51** (III. i. 228)

profess myself: **7** (I. ii. 77)

promised forth: **14** (I. ii. 294)

proof: **23** (II. i. 21)

proper (belonging): **6** (I. ii. 41)

proper (individual): **93** (V. iii. 96)

For students and for teachers, there is something new to learn every day.

Some teachers give private music lessons.

This ballet teacher is showing her students how to dance.

Teachers also help after school. This music teacher is in charge of band practice.

This student wants to be a gymnast. His teacher is helping him train.

This class takes place in a computer lab.

Some teachers help with projects in the library.

Teaching doesn't always take place in the classroom. These children are on a field trip.

In this shop class, students learn to work safely.

This boy hopes the teacher will call on him to give the answer.

They also spend time helping children with their homework.

Teachers help students use computers to learn.

This teacher explains that there are different ways to count. This girl is using an abacus.

Reading time is an important part of the day.

Art class can be fun for everyone.

Teachers work hard to make their classes interesting and fun.

Another busy day is about to begin for students and teachers.

A FIREFLY BOOK

CODMAN SQUARE

MAR - - 2002

Published by Firefly Books Ltd. 2001

Copyright © 2001 Firefly Books Ltd.

First Printing

Canadian Cataloguing in Publication Data

Liebman, Daniel
  I want to be a teacher

ISBN 1-55209-572-X (bound)   ISBN 1-55209-570-3 (pbk.)

1. Teachers – Juvenile literature. I. Title.

LB1775.L53 2001   j371.1   C00-932618-9

Published in Canada in 2001 by
Firefly Books Ltd.
3680 Victoria Park Avenue
Willowdale, Ontario, Canada
M2H 3K1

U.S. Cataloging-in-Publication Data
  (Library of Congress Standards)

Liebman, Daniel
  I want to be a teacher / Dan Liebman. —1st ed.

[24] p. : col. ill. ; cm. –(I want to be)
Summary : Photos and easy-to-read text
describe the job of a teacher.
ISBN 1-55209-572-X (bound)
ISBN 1-55209-570-3 (pbk.)
1. Teachers – Vocational guidance. 2. Occupations
I. Title. II. Series
371.1 dc21   2001   AC   CIP

Published in the United States in 2001 by
Firefly Books (U.S.) Inc.
P.O. Box 1338, Ellicott Station
Buffalo, New York, USA
14205

Photo Credits

© Al Harvey, pages 5, 10, 15, 19, 20
© Photodisc, pages 6, 16, front cover
© Eyewire, pages 7, 23, 24
© First Light/R. Goldman, page 8
© CORBIS/Annie Griffiths, page 9
© First Light/Tom & DeeAnn McCarthy, page 11
© Peter Garfield/The Stock Market, page 12

© CORBIS/Kevin Fleming, page 13
© First Light/P. Coll, page 14
© CORBIS/Angela Hampton, page 17
© First Light/J.L. Pelaez, page 18, back cover
© CORBIS/Lowell Georgia, page 20
© Mug Shots/The Stock Market, page 22

Design by Interrobang Graphic Design Inc.
Printed and bound in Canada by Friesens, Altona, Manitoba

*The Publisher acknowledges the financial support of the Government of Canada through
the Book Publishing Industry Development Program for its publishing activities.*

I WANT TO BE A

Teacher

DAN LIEBMAN

FIREFLY BOOKS

I want to be a Teacher